CW01665874

UK only

£2.25

Enid Blyton's FAMOUS FIVE ANNUAL

Purnell

Five on Kirren Island Again

ISBN 0 361 05312 6
Copyright © 1982 Darrell Waters Limited
'Five On Kirrin Island Again' first published by
Hodder & Stoughton Limited in 1947
Copyright © 1982 Purnell Publishers Limited as to the
artwork and features herein
Published 1982 by Purnell Books, Paulton, Bristol BS18 5LQ
Made and printed in Great Britain by Purnell and Sons
(Book Production) Limited, Paulton, Bristol

Contents

Identikit

Julian
Julian is Anne and Dick's older brother. He is the most practical of the Five and is really their leader. He is very good at sport and is an expert swimmer.

George
George is Anne, Julian and Dick's cousin. She and Anne are at school together. The name George is short for Georgina. In her heart of hearts she would rather be a boy, and her impetuous ways and quick temper get her into all sorts of scrapes. She always ends up laughing, however, as she is really a very good-natured girl.

Anne
Anne is Julian and Dick's sister. She is gentler and more timid than her brothers and her cousin George. She is the cautious one and sometimes stops the others being too reckless.

Timmy
Timmy is a very important member of the Famous Five. He belongs to George, and lives in kennels at her school during term-time, but is beloved by all the children and *always* accompanies them on their adventures.

Dick
Dick is Anne and Julian's brother. He and Julian are at the same school and are close friends, although Julian, being the elder of the two, normally takes the lead in their adventures.

Introduction

Five on Kirrin Island Again is the latest Famous Five Annual. This exciting story, told in picture strip and illustrated narrative, provides another puzzling mystery for the Five to solve.

Included in this annual are features and puzzles, all linked to events in the title story. There are quizzes on islands and the seaside as well as brain-teasing puzzles to test your wits. Find out about castles and small-scale models and discover facts on codes and jackdaws.

Finally, for all adventure seekers, there are survival tips for hiking expeditions.

Chapter 1

A letter for George

'Anne! I've just had a letter from home. Father wants to go and live on my island to do some special work!'

Anne was trying to do some of her prep. in a corner of the common-room when her cousin George came bursting in.

George was not a boy; she was a girl called Georgina, but because she had always wanted to be a boy she insisted on being called George. So George she was. She wore her curly hair cut short, and her bright blue eyes gleamed angrily now as she came towards Anne.

'Anne! I've just had a letter from home—and what do you think? Father wants to go and live on my island to do some special work—and he wants to build a sort of tower or something in the castle yard!'

The other girls looked up in amusement, and Anne held out her hand for the letter that George was waving at her. Everyone knew about the little island off Kirrin Bay that belonged to George. Kirrin Island was a tiny place with an old ruined castle in the middle of it: the home of rabbits and gulls and jackdaws.

It had underground dungeons in which George and her cousins had had one or two amazing adventures. It had once belonged to George's mother, and she had given it to George—and George was very fierce where her precious Kirrin Island was concerned! It was *hers*. Nobody else must live there, or even land there without her permission.

And now, dear me, here was her father proposing to go to her island, and even build some sort of workshop there! George was red with exasperation.

'It's just like grown-ups; they go and give you things and then act as though the things were theirs all the time. I don't *want* Father living on my island, and building nasty messy sheds and things there.'

'Oh George—you know your father is a very famous scientist, who needs to work in peace,' said Anne, taking the letter. 'Surely you can lend him your island for a bit?'

'There are plenty of other places where he can work in peace,' said George. 'Oh dear—I was so hoping we could go and stay there in the Easter hols—take our boat there, and food and everything, just like we've done before. Now we shan't be able to if Father really does go there.'

Anne read the letter. It was from George's mother.

My darling George,

I think I must tell you at once that your father proposes to live on Kirrin Island for some little time in order to finish some very important experiments he is making. He will have to have some kind of building erected there—a sort of tower, I believe. Apparently he needs a place where he can have absolute peace and isolation, and also, for some reason, where there is water all around him. The fact of being surrounded by water is necessary to his experiment.

Now, dear, don't be upset about this. I know that you consider Kirrin Island is your very own, but you must allow your family to share it, especially when it is for something as important as your father's scientific work. Father thinks you will be very pleased indeed to lend him Kirrin Island, but I know your funny feelings about it, so I thought I had better write and tell you, before you arrive home and see him installed there, complete with his tower.'

The letter then went on about other things, but Anne did not bother to read these. She looked at George.

'Oh, George! I don't see why you mind your father borrowing Kirrin Island for a bit! I wouldn't mind *my* father borrowing an island from me—if I was lucky enough to have one!'

'*Your* father would talk to you about it first, and ask your permission, and see if you minded,' said George, sulkily. 'My father never does anything like that. He just does exactly as he likes without asking anybody anything. I really do think he might have written to me himself. He just puts my back up.'

'You've got a back that is very easily put up, George,' said Anne, laughing. 'Don't scowl at me like that. *I'm* not borrowing your island without your gracious permission.'

But George wouldn't smile back. She took her letter and read it again gloomily. 'To think that all my lovely holiday plans are spoilt!' she said. 'You know how super Kirrin Island is at Eastertime—all primroses and gorse and baby rabbits. And you and Julian and Dick were coming to stay, and we haven't stayed together since last summer when we went caravanning.'

'I know. It *is* hard luck!' said Anne. 'It would have been wizard to go and stay on the island these hols. But perhaps your father wouldn't mind if we did? We needn't disturb him.'

'As if living on Kirrin Island with Father there would be the same as living there all by ourselves,' said George, scornfully. 'You know it would be horrid.'

Well yes—Anne didn't think on the whole that Kirrin Island would be much fun with Uncle Quentin there. George's father was such a hot-tempered, impatient man, and when he was in the middle of one of his experiments he was quite unbearable. The least noise upset him.

'Oh dear—how he will yell at the jackdaws to keep quiet, and shout at the noisy gulls!' said Anne, beginning to giggle. 'He won't find Kirrin quite so peaceful as he imagines!'

George gave a watery sort of smile. She folded up the letter and turned away. 'Well, I think it's just the limit,' she said. 'I wouldn't have felt so bad if only Father had asked my permission.'

'He'd never do that!' said Anne. 'It just wouldn't occur to him. Now, George, don't spend the rest of the day brooding over your wrongs, for goodness' sake. Go down to the kennels and fetch Timmy. He'll soon cheer you up.'

Timothy was George's dog, whom she loved with all her heart. He was a big brown mongrel dog, with a ridiculously long tail, and a wide mouth that really seemed to smile. All the four cousins loved him. He was so friendly and loving, so lively and amusing, and he had shared so very many adventures with them all. The five of them had had many happy times together.

George went to get Timmy. Her school allowed the children to keep their own pets. If it hadn't allowed this, it is quite certain that George would not have gone to boarding-school! She could not bear to be parted from Timmy for even a day.

Timmy began to bark excitedly as

She folded up the letter and turned away.

soon as she came near. George lost her sulky look and smiled. Dear Timmy, dear trustable Timmy—he was better than any person! He was always on her side, always her friend whatever she did, and to Timmy there was no one in the world so wonderful as George.

They were soon going through the fields together, and George talked to Timmy as she always did. She told him about her father borrowing Kirrin Island. Timmy agreed with every word she said. He listened as if he understood everything, and not even when a rabbit shot across his path did he leave his mistress's side. Timmy always knew when George was upset.

He gave her hand a few little licks every now and again. By the time that George was back at school again she felt much better. She took Timmy into school with her smuggling him in at a side door. Dogs were not allowed in the school building, but George, like her father, often did exactly as she liked.

She hurried Timmy up to her dormitory. He scuttled under her bed quickly and lay down. His tail thumped the floor gently. He knew what this meant. George wanted the comfort of his nearness that night! He would be able to jump on her bed, when lights were out, and snuggle into the crook of her knees. His brown eyes gleamed with delight.

'Now, lie quiet,' said George, and went out of the room to join the other girls. She found Anne, who was busy writing a letter to her brothers, Julian and Dick, at their boarding-school.

'I've told them about Kirrin Island, and your father wanting to borrow it,' she said. 'Would you like to come and stay with *us*, George, these hols, instead of us coming to Kirrin? Then you won't feel cross all the time because your father is on your island.'

'No thanks,' said George, at once.

'I'm going home. I want to keep an eye on father! I don't want him blowing up Kirrin Island with one of his experiments. You know he's messing about with explosives now, don't you?'

'Ooooh—atom bombs, or things like that?' said Anne.

'I don't know,' said George. 'Anyway, quite apart from keeping an eye on Father and my island, we ought to go and stay at Kirrin to keep Mother company. She'll be all alone if Father's on the island. I suppose he'll take food and everything there.'

'Well, there's one thing, we shan't have to creep about on tiptoe and whisper, if your father isn't at Kirrin Cottage!' said Anne. 'We can be as noisy as we like. Do cheer up, George!'

But it took George quite a long time to get over the fit of gloom caused by her mother's letter. Even having Timmy on her bed each night, till he was discovered by an angry teacher, did not quite make up for her disappointment.

The term ran swiftly on to its end. April came in, with sunshine and showers. Holidays came nearer and nearer! Anne thought joyfully of Kirrin, with its lovely sandy beach, its blue sea, its fishing-boats and its lovely cliffside walks.

Julian and Dick thought longingly of them too. This term both they and the girls broke up on the same day. They could meet in London and travel down to Kirrin together. Hurrah!

The day came at last. Trunks were piled in the hall. Cars arrived to fetch some of the children who lived fairly near. The school coaches drew up to take the others down to the station. There was a terrific noise of yelling and shouting everywhere. The teachers could not make themselves heard in the din.

'Anyone would think that every single child had gone completely mad,' said one of them to another. 'Oh, thank goodness, they're getting into the coaches. George! *Must* you rush along the corridor at sixty miles an hour, with Timmy barking his head off all the time!'

'Yes, I must, I must!' cried George. 'Anne, where are you? Do come and get into the coach. I've got Timmy. He knows it's holidays now. Come on, Tim!'

Down to the station went the singing crowd of children. They piled into the train. 'Bags I this seat! Who's taken my bag? Get out, Hetty, you know you can't bring your dog in here with mine. They fight like anything. Hurrah, the guard's blowing his whistle! We're off!'

The engine pulled slowly out of the station, its long train of carriages behind it, filled to bursting with girls off for their holidays. Through the quiet countryside it went, through small towns and villages, and at last ran through the smoky outskirts of London.

'The boys' train is due in two minutes before ours,' said Anne, leaning out of the window, as the train drew slowly into the London station. 'If it was punctual, they might be on our platform to meet us. Oh look, George, look—there they are!'

George hung out of the window too. 'Hi, Julian!' she yelled. 'Here we are! Hi, Dick, Julian!'

Chapter 2

Back at Kirrin Cottage

They all went to have buns and ginger-beer.

Julian, Dick, Anne, George and Timmy went straightaway to have buns and ginger-beer at the station tea-room. It was good to be all together again. Timmy went nearly mad with joy at seeing the two boys. He kept trying to get on to their knees.

'Look here, Timmy, old thing, I love you very much and I'm jolly glad to see you,' said Dick, 'but that's twice you've upset my ginger-beer all over me. Has he behaved himself this term, George?'

'Fairly well,' said George, considering. 'Hasn't he, Anne? I mean—he only got the joint out of the larder once—and he didn't do so *much* harm to that cushion he chewed—and if people *will* leave their goloshes all over the place nobody can blame Timmy for having a good old game with them.'

'And that was the end of the goloshes, I suppose,' said Julian, with a grin. 'On the whole, Timmy, you have a rather poor report. I'm afraid our Uncle Quentin will not award you the usual twenty-five pence we get for good reports.'

At the mention of her father, George scowled. 'I see George has not lost her pretty scowl,' said Dick, in a teasing voice. 'Dear old George! We shouldn't know her unless she put on that fearsome scowl half a dozen times a day!'

'Oh, she's better than she was,' said Anne hurrying to George's defence at once. George was not so touchy as she had once been, when she was being teased. All the same, Anne knew that there might be sparks flying over her father taking Kirrin Island these holidays, and she didn't want George to fly into a temper too soon!

Julian looked at his cousin. 'I say, old thing, you're not going to take this business of Kirrin Island too much to heart, are you?' he said. 'You've just got to realise that your father's a remarkably clever man, one of the finest scientists we've got—and *I* think that those kind of fellows ought to be allowed as much freedom as they like, for their work. I mean—if Uncle Quentin wants to work on Kirrin Island for some peculiar reason of his own, then you ought to be pleased to say "Go ahead, Father!"'

George looked a little mutinous after this rather long speech; but she thought a great deal of Julian, and usually went by what he said. He was older than any of them, a tall, good-looking boy, with determined eyes and a strong chin. George scratched Timmy's head, and spoke in a low voice.

'All right. I won't go up in smoke about it, Julian. But I'm frightfully disappointed. I'd planned to go to Kirrin Island ourselves these hols.'

'Well, we're all disappointed,' said Julian. 'Buck up with your bun, old thing. We've got to get across London and catch the train for Kirrin. We shall miss it if we don't hurry ourselves up.'

Julian found them all corner seats in the carriage.

Aunt Fanny was at the station to meet them.

Soon they were in the train for Kirrin. Julian was very good at getting porters and taxis. Anne gazed admiringly at her big brother as he found them all corner-seats in a carriage. Julian did know how to tackle things!

'Do you think I've grown, Julian?' she asked him. 'I did hope I'd be as tall as George by the end of this term, but she grew too!'

'Well, I should think you might be a quarter of an inch taller than last term,' said Julian. 'You can't catch us up, Anne—you'll always be the smallest! But I like you small.'

'Look at Timmy, putting his head out of the window as usual!' said Dick. 'Timmy, you'll get grit in your eye. Then George will go quite mad with grief and think you're going blind!'

'Woof,' said Timmy, and wagged his tail. That was the nice part about Timmy. He always knew when he was being spoken to, even if his name was not mentioned, and he answered at once.

Aunt Fanny was at the station to meet them in the pony-trap. The children flung themselves on her, for they were very fond of her. She was kind and gentle, and did her best to keep her clever, impatient husband from finding too much fault with the children.

'How's Uncle Quentin?' asked Julian, politely, when they were setting off in the trap.

'He's very well,' said his aunt. 'And terribly excited. Really, I've never known him to be so thrilled as he has been lately. His work has been coming along very successfully.'

'I suppose you don't know what his latest experiment is?' said Dick.

'Oh no. He never tells me a word,' said Aunt Fanny. 'He never tells anyone anything while he is at work, except his colleagues, of course. But I do know it's very important—and I know, of course, that the last part of the experiment has to be made in a place where there is deep water all around. Don't ask me why! I don't know.'

'Look! There's Kirrin Island!' said Anne, suddenly. They had rounded a corner, and had come in sight of the bay. Guarding the entrance to it was the curious little island topped

The sun shone down on the blue sea, and the island looked most enchanting.

by the old ruined castle. The sun shone down on the blue sea, and the island looked most enchanting.

George looked earnestly at it. She was looking for the building, whatever it was, that her father said he needed for his work. Everyone looked at the island, seeking the same thing.

They saw it easily enough! Rising from the centre of the castle, probably from the castle yard, was a tall thin tower, rather like a lighthouse. At the top was a glass-enclosed room, which glittered in the sun.

'Oh, Mother! I don't like it! It spoils Kirrin Island,' said George, in dismay.

'Darling, it can come down when your father has finished his work,' said her mother. 'It's a very flimsy, temporary thing. It can easily be pulled down. Father promised me he would scrap it as soon as his work was done. He says you can go across and see it, if you like. It's really rather interesting.'

'Ooooh—I'd *love* to go and see it,' said Anne, at once. 'It looks so queer. Is Uncle Quentin all alone on Kirrin Island, Aunt Fanny?'

'Yes, I don't like him to be alone,' said her aunt. 'For one thing I am sure he doesn't get his meals properly, and for another, I'm always afraid some harm might come to him when he's experimenting—and if he's alone, how would I know if anything happened to him?'

'Well, Aunt Fanny, you could always arrange for him to signal to you each morning and night, couldn't you?' said Julian, sensibly. 'He could use that tower easily. He could flash a signal to you in the morning, using a mirror, you know—heliographing that he was all right—and at night he could signal with a lamp. Easy!'

'Yes. I did suggest that sort of thing,' said his aunt. 'I said I'd go over with you all tomorrow, to see him and perhaps, Julian dear, you could arrange something of the sort with your uncle? He seems to listen to you now.'

'Gracious! Do you mean to say Father wants us to invade his secret lair, and actually to see his strange tower?' asked George, surprised. 'Well—I don't think I want to go. After all, it's *my* island—and it's horrid to see someone else taking possession of it.'

'Oh, George, don't begin all that again,' said Anne, with a sigh. 'You and your island! Can't you even *lend* it to your own father! Aunt Fanny, you should have seen George when your letter came. She looked so fierce that I was quite scared!'

Everyone laughed except George and Aunt Fanny. She looked distressed. George was always so difficult! She found fault with her father, and got up against him time after time—but dear me, how very, very like him she was, with her scowls, her sudden temper, and her fierceness! If only George was as sweet-tempered and as easy-going as these three cousins of hers!

George looked at her mother's

troubled face, and felt ashamed of herself. She put her hand on her knee. 'It's all right, Mother! I won't make a fuss. I'll try and keep my feelings to myself, really I will. I know Father's work is important. I'll go with you to the island tomorrow.'

Julian gave George a gentle clap on the back. 'Good old George! She's actually learned, not only to give in, but to give in gracefully! George, you're more like a boy than ever when you act like that.'

George glowed. She liked Julian to say she was like a boy. She didn't want to be petty and catty and bear malice as so many girls did. But Anne looked a little indignant.

'It isn't *only* boys that can learn to give in decently, and things like that,' she said. 'Heaps of girls do. Well, I jolly well hope I do myself!'

'My goodness, here's another firebrand!' said Aunt Fanny, smiling. 'Stop arguing now, all of you—here's Kirrin Cottage. Doesn't it look sweet with all the primroses in the garden, and the wallflowers coming out, and the daffodils peeping everywhere?'

It certainly did. The four children and Timmy tore in at the front gate, delighted to be back. They clattered into the house, and, to their great delight, found Joanna, the old cook there. She had come back to help for the holidays. She beamed at the children, and fondled Timmy when he leapt round her barking.

'Well, there now! Haven't you all grown again? How big you are, Master Julian—taller than I am, I declare. And little Miss Anne, why, she's getting quite big.'

That pleased Anne, of course. Julian went back to the front door to help his aunt with the small bags in the trap. The trunks were coming later. Julian and Dick took everything upstairs.

Anne joined them, eager to see her old bedroom again. Oh, how good it was to be in Kirrin Cottage once more! She looked out of the windows. One looked on to the moor at the back. The other looked sideways on to the sea. Lovely! Lovely! She began to sing a little song as she undid her bag.

'You know,' she said to Dick, when he brought George's bag in, 'you know, Dick, I'm really quite pleased that Uncle Quentin has gone to Kirrin Island, even if it means we won't be able to go there much! I feel much freer in the house when he's away. He's a very clever man and he can be awfully nice—but I always feel a bit afraid of him.'

Dick laughed. 'I'm not afraid of him—but he's a bit of a wet blanket in a house, I must say, when we're here for the holidays. Funny to think of him on Kirrin Island all alone.'

A voice came up the stairs. 'Come down to tea, because there are hot scones for you, just out of the oven.'

'Coming, Aunt Fanny!' called Dick. 'Hurry, Anne. I'm awfully hungry. Julian, did you hear Aunt Fanny calling?'

George came up the stairs to fetch Anne. She was pleased to be home, and as for Timmy, he was engaged in going round every single corner of the house, sniffing vigorously.

'He always does that!' said George. 'As if he thought that there *might* be a chair or a table that didn't smell quite the same as it always did. Come on, Tim. Teatime! Mother, as Father isn't here, can Timmy sit beside me on the floor? He's awfully well-behaved now.'

'Very well,' said her mother, and tea began. What a tea! It looked as if it was a spread for a party of twenty. Good old Joanna! She must have baked all day. Well, there wouldn't be much left when the Five had finished!

The four children and Timmy tore in at the front gate, delighted to be back.

Introducing Islands

Kilauea volcano erupts on Hawaii.

What do you think of when you read the word, island? Close your eyes and see what picture comes to mind.

Is it a desert island in the middle of the ocean — a little piece of land topped by a lonely palm tree and perhaps a lonely shipwrecked sailor too? Or is it lots of small islands just off the mainland, like those on the west coast of Scotland? Maybe it's an island in a different country that you have visited on holiday, such as Majorca, Minorca, Capri, or even the West Indies. Perhaps, because you are reading this book right now, you see Kirrin Island. It is not so likely, but you may visualise a large country such as Greenland when you think of an island.

There are so many different kinds of island, and each has its own characteristics. The Five obviously think of Kirrin Island as something rather special, and of course George looks upon it as being her very own. A piece of land, large or small, with water all round it seems to hold a certain fascination for almost everyone. It can be a world of its own. Think how tame the rabbits are on Kirrin Island, where they are not used to being invaded by Timmy or any of his four-legged friends.

Unusual animals and birds have often developed on isolated islands — creatures that are not seen anywhere else. Many of them would probably die out elsewhere. They survive on islands because there are fewer animals to prey on them, and there is less competition for food. In the Galapagos Islands, for instance, there are giant tortoises and lizards that are unique to the islands.

Not all islands are islands for the same reason, of course, but they are usually referred to as one of two main kinds, which are continental and oceanic.

Oceanic islands, which are far more numerous, were never connected to a continent. In fact, they are often thousands of miles from the mainland. They may be *volcanic* islands, consisting of lava built up from the bottom of the ocean. Not all submerged volcanoes eventually reach the surface of the ocean, but many do rise abruptly out of the sea to form high islands. The Hawaiian Islands are the result of volcanic eruptions that began three miles below the surface of the ocean.

Other oceanic islands are low flat islands made of *coral.* These have been built up by tiny sea animals known as coral polyps, which live in colonies and thrive in warm shallow water. They grow on the skeletons of dead polyps and as they live and die in turn they gradually build up an accumulation of coral.

The coral eventually forms one of three kinds of reef. A *fringing* reef is found around an island (sometimes a volcanic island) or the shore of a continent. If the land slowly sinks or the sea level rises, the reef may grow up to form a *barrier* reef. It has then become further away from the mainland and divided by a deeper sea. If the land submerges completely, it may leave a lagoon inside a ring of coral known as an *atoll*.

When you consider that these oceanic islands have gradually grown up from nothing, it is not surprising that they originally had no land animals or birds of their own. So the creatures that inhabit oceanic islands now are generally birds that fly across the sea, and animals and insects that swim there or are transported on logs and other debris. The plants grow from seeds carried by birds or ocean currents. They usually thrive well on these islands, but there isn't the large variety of plants found on the mainland.

Continental islands are really portions of larger lands which have been cut off by the sea. They are generally close to the mainland and divided by a comparatively shallow sea. Some resulted from a rise in sea level, others from a sinking of the land. If the sinking land is mountainous, the sea may fill the valleys leaving the tops of the submerged mountains as small islands or peninsulas. This is how many of the islands off the west coast of Scotland and Canada were formed. Continental islands are obviously very much like the mainland from which they have become separated, and so usually have similar plants and animals.

Apart from their unusual plant and animal life, islands can be significant for many other reasons. Some islands have developed into large cities, because their location provides protection and security. Venice, Hong Kong and Singapore are typical examples. Others have been used as isolation centres, on which to keep dangerous criminals, or people suffering from serious contagious diseases. Some are important naval bases or refuelling stations for ships or aeroplanes. There are a few islands, such as Cuba near the United States, that are conveniently situated off the shores of a political rival.

Some islands, like Java and Hong Kong, are heavily populated. Others, like most of the Arctic and Antarctic islands and tiny coral islands, have little or no human habitation.

To anyone other than the four children and Timmy there was nothing specially significant about Kirrin Island. But when George's father needed somewhere quiet and completely private to work on his experiment, Kirrin Island became very important indeed. He needed an island on which to escape from the rest of the world. And that is what islands are often all about.

Chapter 3

Off to Kirrin Island

IT'S THE LITTLE ROOM AT THE TOP THAT IS IMPORTANT. NOT THAT YOUR UNCLE **DOES** ANYTHING WITH THE TOWER — IT JUST HAS TO BE THERE FOR HIS EXPERIMENTS.
I SHOULD LIKE TO GO UP THE TOWER.
WELL, PERHAPS YOUR UNCLE WILL LET YOU.
OH, LOOK AT THE RABBITS — AREN'T THEY LOVELY!
TIMMY'S SEEN THEM, TOO! NOW, TIMMY, DON'T GO CHASING THEM ALL AWAY!
BUT THE SIGHT OF THE RABBITS HAD BEEN TOO MUCH FOR POOR TIMMY — HE'D LOST ALL SELF-CONTROL!
TIMMY!
GEORGE'S VOICE WAS CROSS THIS TIME — AND TIMMY SLID TO A HALT, TURNING A DESPAIRING EYE ON HIS MISTRESS. 'WHAT!' HE SEEMED TO SAY. 'NOT EVEN A SCAMPER AFTER THE RABBITS? HOW HARD-HEARTED GEORGE COULD BE!'
THEY WENT UP INTO THE OLD RUINED CASTLE, WONDERING WHERE UNCLE QUENTIN WAS...
I SUPPOSE YOUR FATHER LIVES IN THE LITTLE OLD ROOM WITH THE TWO SLIT-LIKE WINDOWS, GEORGE.
WELL, THAT'S THE ONLY PLACE THAT WOULD GIVE HIM SHELTER. EVERYWHERE ELSE IS IN RUINS. DO YOU REMEMBER WE ONCE SPENT A NIGHT THERE?
YES, IT WAS FUN! I SUPPOSE THERE'S NOWHERE ELSE WHERE YOUR FATHER COULD BE — UNLESS HE'S DOWN IN THE DUNGEONS!
OH, NO-ONE WOULD LIVE IN THE DUNGEONS — THEY'RE SO DARK AND COLD. WHERE **IS** YOUR FATHER, GEORGE? I CAN'T SEE HIM ANYWHERE.
MOTHER, WHERE WOULD FATHER BE? WHERE'S HIS WORKSHOP — IN THAT OLD ROOM THERE?
WELL, REALLY, I DON'T EXACTLY KNOW...
HE'S ALWAYS MET ME DOWN AT THE COVE, AND WE'VE JUST SAT ON THE SAND AND HAD A PICNIC AND TALKED. HE DIDN'T SEEM TO WANT ME TO POKE ROUND MUCH.

LET'S CALL HIM. UNCLE QUENTIN UNCLE QUENTIN! WHERE ARE YOU?
THE JACKDAWS FLEW UP IN FRIGHT, AND A FEW GULLS JOINED IN THE CRY OF ALARM– BUT NO UNCLE QUENTIN APPEARED!
UNCLE QUENTIN! WHERE ARE YOU?
UNCLE QUENTIN!
WHAT A NOISE! I SHOULD THINK JOANNA MUST HAVE HEARD THAT AT HOME. OH DEAR– WHERE IS YOUR UNCLE?
OH WELL– HE MUST BE SOMEWHERE ABOUT. I EXPECT HE'S DEEP IN SOME BOOK OR OTHER. WE'LL HUNT FOR HIM.
YES. WE'LL LOOK IN THAT LITTLE DARK ROOM.
BUT...
HE'S NOT HERE! AND WHAT'S MORE– THERE'S NOTHING HERE AT ALL!
NO FOOD, NO CLOTHES, NO STORES OF ANY SORT. THIS IS NOT HIS WORK-ROOM, NOR EVEN HIS STORE!
THEN HE MUST BE DOWN IN THE DUNGEONS. PERHAPS IT'S NECESSARY TO HIS WORK TO BE UNDERGROUND– AND WITH WATER ALL ROUND! COME ON– WE KNOW WHERE THE ENTRANCE IS.
YES, HE MUST BE IN THE DUNGEONS. ARE YOU COMING DOWN, MOTHER?
OH NO. I CAN'T BEAR THOSE DUNGEONS. I'LL SIT OUT HERE IN THE SUN AND UNPACK THE SANDWICHES. IT'S ALMOST LUNCH-TIME.
THE ENTRANCE TO THE DUNGEONS WAS NEAR THE OLD WELL IN THE MIDDLE OF THE YARD...
THAT'S ODD– I THOUGHT IT MIGHT BE OPEN, SO THAT WE COULD COULD GO DOWN THE STEPS. OH WELL...
AND THEN SOME-THING VERY STRANGE...
LOOK– THERE ARE WEEDS GROWING ROUND THE EDGES OF THE STONE. NOBODY HAS LIFTED IT FOR A LONG TIME. UNCLE QUENTIN ISN'T DOWN IN THE DUNGEONS!
THEN WHERE IS HE? WHEREVER CAN HE BE?

Chapter 4
Where is Uncle Quentin?

The four of them, with Timmy nosing round their legs, stood staring down at the big stone that hid the entrance to the dungeons. Julian was perfectly right. The stone could not have been lifted for months, because weeds had grown closely round the edges, sending their small roots into every crack.

'No one is down there,' said Julian. 'We need not even bother to pull up the stone and go down to see. If it had been lifted lately, those weeds would have been torn up as it was raised.'

'And anyway, we know that no one can get *out* of the dungeon once the entrance stone is closing it,' said Dick. 'It's too heavy. Uncle Quentin wouldn't be silly enough to shut himself in! He'd leave it open.'

'Of course he would,' said Anne. 'Well—he's not there, then. He must be somewhere else.'

'But *where*?' said George. 'This is only a small island, and we know every corner of it. Oh—would he be in that cave we hid in once? The only cave on the island.'

'Oh yes—he might be,' said Julian. 'But I doubt it. I can't see Uncle Quentin dropping down through the hole in the cave's roof—and that's the only way of getting into it unless you're going to clamber and slide about the rocks on the shore for ages. I can't see him doing that, either.'

They made their way beyond the castle to the other side of the island. Here there was a cave they had once lived in. It could be entered with difficulty on the seaward side, as Julian had said, by clambering over slippery rocks, or it could be entered by dropping down a rope through a hole in the roof to the floor some way below.

'I'll slide down and have a look,' Julian said.

They found the hole, half hidden in old heather. Julian felt about. The rope was still there. 'I'll slide down and have a look,' he said.

He went down the rope. It was knotted at intervals so that his feet found holding-places and he did not slide down too quickly and scorch his hands.

He was soon in the cave. A dim light came in from the seaward side. Julian took a quick look round. There was absolutely nothing there at all, except for an old box that they must have left behind when they were last here themselves.

He climbed up the rope again, his head appearing suddenly out of the hole. Dick gave him a hand.

'Well?' he said. 'Any sign of Uncle Quentin?'

'No,' said Julian. 'He's not there, and hasn't been there either, I should think. It's a mystery! Where is he, and if he's really doing important work where is all his stuff? I mean, we know that plenty of stuff was brought here, because Aunt Fanny told us so.'

'Do you think he's in the tower?' said Anne, suddenly. 'He might be in that glass room at the top.'

'Well, he'd see us at once, if he were!' said Julian, scornfully. '*And* hear our yells too! Still, we might as well have a look.'

So back to the castle they went and walked to the queer tower.

Their aunt saw them and called to them. 'Your lunch is ready. Come and have it. Your uncle will turn up, I expect.'

'But Aunt Fanny where is he?' said Anne, with a puzzled face. 'We've looked simply *every*where!'

Her aunt did not know the island as well as the children did. She imagined that there were plenty of places to shelter in, or to work in. 'Never mind,' she said, looking quite undisturbed. 'He'll turn up later. You come along and have your meal.'

'We think we'll go up the tower,' said Julian. 'Just in case he's up there working.'

The four children and Timmy went to where the tower rose up from the castle yard. They ran their hands over the smooth, shining sections, which were fitted together in curving rows. 'What's this stuff it's built of?' said Dick.

'Some kind of new plastic material, I should think,' said Julian. 'Very light and strong, and easily put together.'

'I should be afraid it would blow down in a gale,' said George.

'Yes, so should I,' said Dick. 'Look—here is the door.'

The door was small, and rounded at the top. A key was in the keyhole. Julian turned it and unlocked the door. It opened outwards not inwards. Julian put his head inside and looked round.

There was not much room in the tower. A spiral staircase, made of the same shiny stuff as the tower itself, wound up and up and up. There was a space at one side of it, into which projected curious hook-like objects made of what looked like steel. Wire ran from one to the other.

'Better not touch them.' said Julian, looking curiously at them. 'Goodness, this is like a tower out of a fairy-tale. Come on—I'm going up the stairs to the top.'

He began to climb the steep, spiral stairway. It made him quite giddy to go up and round, up and round so many, many times.

They went to where the tower rose up from the castle yard.

The others followed him. Tiny, slit-like windows, set sideways not downwards, were let into the side of the tower here and there, and gave a little light to the stairway. Julian looked through one, and had a wonderful view of the sea and the mainland.

He went on up to the top. When he got there he found himself in a small round room, whose sides were of thick, gleaming glass. Wires ran right into the glass itself, and then pierced through it, the free ends waving and glittering in the strong wind that blew round the tower.

There was nothing in the little room at all! Certainly Uncle Quentin was not there. It was clearly only a tower meant to take the wires up on the hook-like things, and to run them through the strange, thick glass at the top, and set them free in the air. What for? Were they catching some kind of wireless waves? Was it to do with Radar? Julian wondered, frowning, what was the meaning of the tower and the thin, shining wires?

The others crowded into the little room. Timmy came too, having managed the spiral stairs with great difficulty.

'Gracious! What a queer place!' said George. 'My goodness, what a view we've got from here. We can see miles and miles out to sea—and on this other side we can see miles and miles across the bay, over the mainland to the hills beyond.'

'Yes. It's lovely,' said Anne. 'But —*where* is Uncle Quentin? We still haven't found him. I suppose he *is* on the island.'

'Well, his boat was pulled up in the cove,' said George. 'We saw it.'

'Then he must be here somewhere,' said Dick. 'But he's not in the castle, he's not in the dungeons, he's not in the cave and he's not up here. It's a first-class mystery.'

'The Missing Uncle. Where is he?' said Julian. 'Look, there's poor Aunt Fanny still down there, waiting with the lunch. We'd better go down. She's signalling to us.'

'I should like to,' said Anne. 'It's an awful squash in this tiny glass room. I say—did you feel the tower sway then, when that gust of wind shook it? I'm going down quickly, before the whole thing blows over!'

She began to go down the spiral

stairs, holding on to a little hand-rail that ran down beside them. The stairs were so steep that she was afraid of falling. She nearly *did* fall when Timmy pushed his way past her, and disappeared below at a remarkably fast pace.

Soon they were all down at the bottom. Julian locked the door again. 'Not much good locking a door if you leave the key in,' he said. 'Still—I'd better.'

They walked over to Aunt Fanny. 'Well, I thought you were never coming!' she said. 'Did you see anything interesting up there?'

'Only a lovely view,' said Anne. 'Simply magnificent. But we didn't find Uncle Quentin. It's very mysterious, Aunt Fanny—we really have looked everywhere on the island—but he's just not here.'

'And yet his boat is in the cove,' said Dick. 'So he can't have gone.'

'Yes, it does sound queer,' said Aunt Fanny, handing round the sandwiches. 'But you don't know your uncle as well as I do. He always turns up all right. He's forgotten I was bringing you, or he would be here. As it is, we may not see him, if he's quite forgotten about your coming. If he remembers, he'll suddenly turn up.'

'But where from?' asked Dick, munching a potted meat sandwich. 'He's done a jolly good disappearing trick, Aunt Fanny.'

'Well, you'll see where he comes from, I've no doubt, when he arrives,' said Aunt Fanny. 'Another sandwich, George? No, *not* you, Timmy. You've had three already. Oh George, do keep Timmy's head out of that plate.'

'He's hungry too, Mother,' said George.

'Well, I've brought dog-biscuits for him,' said her mother.

'Oh, Mother! As if Timmy would eat *dog* biscuits when he can have sandwiches,' said George. 'He only eats dog biscuits when there's absolutely nothing else and he's so ravenous he can't help eating them.'

'Well, I thought you were never coming!' she said.

They sat in the warm April sunshine, eating hungrily.

They sat in the warm April sunshine, eating hungrily. There was orangeade to drink, cool and delicious. Timmy wandered over to a rock pool he knew, where rainwater collected, and he could be heard lapping there.

'Hasn't he got a good memory?' said George proudly. 'It's ages since he was here—and yet he remembered that pool at once, when he felt thirsty.'

'It's funny Timmy hasn't found Uncle Quentin, isn't it?' said Dick, suddenly. 'I mean—when we were hunting for him, and got "Warm" you'd think Timmy would bark or scrape about or something. But he didn't.'

'I think it's jolly funny that Father can't be found anywhere,' said George. 'I do really. I can't think how you can take it so calmly, Mother.'

'Well, dear, as I said before, I know your father better than you do,' said her mother. 'He'll turn up in his own good time. Why, I remember once when he was doing some sort of work in the stalactite caves at Cheddar, he disappeared in them for over a week—but he wandered out all right when he had finished his experiments.'

'It's very queer,' began Anne, and then stopped suddenly. A curious noise came to their ears—a rumbling, grumbling, angry noise, like a giant hidden dog, growling in fury. Then there was a hissing noise from the tower, and all the wires that waved at the top were suddenly lit up as if by lightning.

'There now—I knew your father was somewhere about,' said George's mother. 'I heard that noise when I was here before—but I couldn't make out where it came from.'

'Where *did* it come from?' said Dick. 'It sounded almost as if it was underneath us, but it couldn't have been. Gracious, this is most mysterious.'

No more noises came. They each helped themselves to buns with jam in the middle. And then Anne gave a squeal that made them all jump violently.

'Look! *There's* Uncle Quentin! Standing over there, near the tower. He's watching the jackdaws! Wherever *did* he come from?'

'Look! There's Uncle Quentin!'

Jaunty Jackdaws

'Chack, chack, chack,' cried the cloud of jackdaws as they rose up into the air and circled round the old ruined castle on Kirrin Island. Maybe they were objecting to the possible invasion of their homes by the arrival of George and her cousins.

Jackdaws are very sociable birds. They always nest in colonies, and fly around in groups, often in the company of starlings, rooks or crows. Jackdaws are more lively than the larger members of the crow family, and are easily recognised by the grey on the back of their head and neck. The rest of their plumage is black, and they have a much shorter bill than a crow.

The ruined castle tower on Kirrin Island made an ideal home for them as jackdaws are very fond of nesting in old buildings, and holes in trees, cliffs and quarries. Sometimes they choose a chimney, but this can have rather unfortunate consequences. Having stuffed vast quantities of twigs for their nest into the chimney, the jackdaws or their young are liable to fall down into the room below.

They are not content to line their nests with straw and feathers either. Jackdaws take great delight in rummaging in litterbins for old paper bags and other rubbish. Some even perch on the backs of farm animals and pull out tufts of hair.

They lay four to six light blue-green eggs with brown spots, and these eggs hatch after about eighteen days. The nestlings are fed by both parents on a diet of grubs and insects. The adults also eat other small creatures and seeds, and soft fruits.

The young jackdaws leave the nest when they are a month old, and are soon seen flying around the neighbourhood.

These are easy birds to tame and make very interesting pets. If it is removed from the colony, a jackdaw soon becomes fond of its owner and will stay with him even if it has the opportunity to fly away. It likes to imitate human sounds, and by the time it is a year old, a jackdaw can talk quite clearly. They are quite simple to feed, especially if you can provide a dish of macaroni-cheese at lunchtime!

Chapter 5

A mystery

Everyone stared at Uncle Quentin. There he was, intently watching the jackdaws, his hands in his pockets. He hadn't seen the children or his wife.

Timmy leapt to his feet, and gambolled over to George's father. He barked loudly. Uncle Quentin jumped and turned round. He saw Timmy—and then he saw all the others, staring at him in real astonishment.

Uncle Quentin did not look particularly pleased to see anyone. He walked slowly over to them, a slight frown on his face. 'This *is* a surprise,' he said. 'I had no idea you were all coming today.'

'Oh, *Quentin*!' said his wife, reproachfully. 'I wrote it down for you in your diary. You know I did.'

'Did you! Well, I haven't looked at my diary since, so it's no wonder I forgot,' said Uncle Quentin, a little peevishly. He kissed his wife, George and Anne, and shook hands with the boys.

'Uncle Quentin—where did you come from?' asked Dick, who was eaten up with curiosity. 'We've looked for you for ages.'

'Oh, I was in my workroom,' said Uncle Quentin, vaguely.

'Well, but where's that?' demanded Dick. 'Honestly, Uncle, we can't imagine where you hide yourself. We even went up the tower to see if you were in that funny glass room at the top.'

'*What!*' exploded his uncle, in a sudden surprising fury. 'You dared to go up there? You might have been in great danger. I've just finished an experiment, and all those wires in there were connected with it.'

'Yes, we saw them acting a bit queerly,' said Julian.

'You've no business to come over here, and interfere with my work,' said his uncle, still looking furious. 'How did you get into that tower? I locked it.'

'Yes, it was locked all right,' said Julian. 'But you left the key in, you see, Uncle—so I thought it wouldn't matter if . . .'

'Oh, that's where the key is, is it?' said his uncle. 'I thought I'd lost it. Well, don't you ever go into that tower again. I tell you, it's dangerous.'

'Uncle Quentin, you haven't told us yet where your workroom is,' said Dick, who was quite determined to know. 'We can't imagine where you suddenly came from.'

'I told them you would turn up, Quentin,' said his wife. 'You look a bit thin, dear. Have you been having regular meals? You know, I left you plenty of good soup to heat up.'

'Did you?' said her husband. 'Well, I don't know if I've had it or not. I don't worry about meals when I'm working. I'll have some of those sandwiches now, though, if nobody else wants them.'

He began to devour the sandwiches, one after another, as if he was ravenous. Aunt Fanny watched him in distress.

'Oh, Quentin—you're starving. I shall come over here and stay and look after you!'

Her husband looked alarmed. 'Oh no! Nobody is to come here. I can't have my work interfered with. I'm working on an extremely important discovery.'

'Is it a discovery that nobody else knows about?' asked Anne, her eyes wide with admiration. How clever Uncle Quentin was!

'Well—I'm not sure about that,'

Uncle Quentin jumped and turned round.

said Uncle Quentin, taking two sandwiches at once. 'That's partly why I came over here—besides the fact that I wanted water round me and above me. I have a feeling that somebody knows a bit more than I want them to know. But there's one thing—they can't come here unless they're shown the way through all those rocks that lie round the island. Only a few of the fishermen know that, and they've been given orders not to bring anyone here at all. I think you're the only other person that knows the way, George.'

'Uncle Quentin—please do tell us where your workroom is,' begged Dick, feeling that he could not wait a single moment more to solve the mystery.

'Don't keep bothering your uncle,' said his aunt, annoyingly. 'Let him eat his lunch. He can't have had anything for ages!'

'Yes, but Aunt Fanny, I . . .' began Dick and was interrupted by his uncle.

'You obey your aunt, young man. I don't want to be pestered by any of you. What does it matter where I work?'

'Oh, it doesn't really matter a bit, sir,' said Dick, hurriedly. 'It's only that I'm awfully curious to know. You see, we looked for you simply everywhere.'

'Well, you're not quite so clever as you thought you were then,' said Uncle Quentin, and reached for a jammy bun. 'George, take this dog of yours away from me. He keeps breathing down my neck, hoping I shall give him a tit-bit. I don't approve of tit-bits at meal-times.'

George pulled Timmy away. Her mother watched her father gobbling up the rest of the food. Most of the sandwiches she had saved for tea-time had gone already. Poor Quentin! How very hungry he must be.

'Quentin, you don't think there's any danger for you here, do you?' she said. 'I mean—you don't think anyone would try to come spying on you, as they did once before?'

'How will you signal! Will you flash with a mirror!'

'No. How could they?' said her husband. 'No plane can land on this island. No boat can get through the rocks unless the way through is known, and the sea's too rough round the rocks for any swimmer.'

'Julian, see if you can make him promise to signal to me night and morning,' said Aunt Fanny, turning to her nephew. 'I feel worried about him somehow.'

Julian tackled his uncle manfully. 'Uncle, it wouldn't be too much of a bother to you to signal to Aunt Fanny twice a day, would it?'

'If you don't, Quentin, I shall come over every single day to see you,' said his wife.

'And we might come too,' said Anne mischievously. Her uncle looked most dismayed at the idea.

'Well, I could signal in the morning and in the evening when I go up to the top of the tower,' he said, 'I have to go up once every twelve hours to re-adjust the wires. I'll signal then. Half past ten in the morning and half past ten at night.'

'How will you signal?' asked Julian. 'Will you flash with a mirror in the morning?'

'Yes—that would be quite a good idea,' said his uncle. 'I could do that easily. And I'll use a lantern at night. I'll shine it out six times at half past ten. Then perhaps you'll all know I'm all right and will leave me alone! But don't look for the signal tonight. I'll start tomorrow morning.'

'Oh, Quentin dear, you do sound cross,' said his wife. 'I don't like you being all alone here, that's all. You look thin and tired. I'm sure you're not . . .'

Uncle Quentin put on a scowl exactly like George sometimes put on. He looked at his wrist-watch. 'Well, I must go,' he said. 'Time to get to work again. I'll see you to your boat.'

'We're going to stay to tea here, Father,' said George.

'No, I'd rather you didn't,' said her father, getting up. 'Come on—I'll take you to your boat.'

'But Father—I haven't been on my island for ages!' said George, indignantly. 'I want to stay here a bit longer. I don't see why I shouldn't.'

'Well, I've had enough interruption to my work,' said her father. 'I want to get on.'

'We shan't disturb you, Uncle Quentin,' said Dick, who was still terribly curious to know where his uncle had his workroom. Why wouldn't he tell them! Was he just being annoying? Or didn't he want them to know?

Uncle Quentin led them all firmly towards the little cove. It was plain that he meant them to go and to go quickly.

'When shall we come over and see you again, Quentin?' asked his wife.

'Not till I say so,' said her husband. 'It won't take me long now to finish what I'm on. My word, that dog's got a rabbit at last!'

'Oh, *Timmy*!' yelled George in distress. Timmy dropped the rabbit

Julian cupped his hands round his mouth. 'Don't forget to signal, sir!'

he had actually managed to grab. It scampered away unhurt. Timmy came to his mistress looking very sheepish.

'You're a very bad dog. Just because I took my eye off you for half a second! No, it's no good licking my hand like that. I'm cross.'

They all came to the boat. 'I'll push her off,' said Julian. 'Get in, all of you. Well, good-bye, Uncle Quentin. I hope your work goes well.'

Everyone got into the boat. Timmy tried to put his head on George's knee, but she pushed it away.

'Oh, be kind to him and forgive him,' begged Anne. 'He looks as if he's going to cry.'

'Are you ready?' cried Julian. 'Got the oars, George? Dick, take the other pair.'

He shoved the boat off and leapt in himself. He cupped his hands round his mouth. 'Don't forget to signal, sir! We'll be watching out morning and evening!'

'And if you forget, you can be sure I shall come over the very next day!' called his wife.

The boat slid away down the little inlet of water, and Uncle Quentin was lost to sight. Then round the low wall of rocks went the boat, and was soon on the open sea.

'Ju, watch and see if you can make out where Uncle Quentin is, when we're round these rocks,' said Dick. 'See what direction he goes in.'

Julian tried to see his uncle, but the rocks just there hid the cove from sight, and there was no sign of him at all.

'*Why* didn't he want us to stay? Because he didn't want us to know his hiding-place!' said Dick. 'And *why* doesn't he want us to know? Because it's somewhere *we* don't know, either!'

'But I thought we knew every single corner of my island,' said George. 'I think it's mean of Father not to tell me, if it's somewhere I don't know. I can't think *where* it can be!'

Timmy put his head on her knee again. George was so absorbed in trying to think where her father's hiding place could be that she absent-mindedly stroked Timmy's head. He was almost beside himself with delight. He licked her fingers lovingly.

'Oh, Timmy— I didn't mean to pet you for ages,' said George. 'Stop licking my hands. You make them feel wet and horrid. Dick, it's very mysterious, isn't it—where *can* Father be hiding?'

'I can't imagine,' said Dick. He looked back at the island. A cloud of jackdaws rose up into the air calling loudly, 'Chack, chack, chack!'

The boy watched them. What had disturbed them? Was it Uncle Quentin? Perhaps his hiding-place was somewhere about that old tower then, the one the jackdaws nested in? On the other hand, the jackdaws often rose into the air together for no reason at all.

'Those jackdaws are making a bit of fuss,' he said. 'Perhaps Uncle's hiding-place is not far from where they roost together, by that tower.'

'Can't be,' said Julian. 'We went all round there today.'

'Well, it's a mystery,' said George, gloomily, 'and I think it's horrible having a mystery about my very own island—and to be forbidden to go to it, and solve it. It's really *too* bad you know!'

Chapter 6

Up on the cliff

I'VE GOT NEW NEIGHBOURS IN THE NEXT COTTAGE — MAN AND A BOY — AND THE MAN'S BEEN BUYING ALL THE TOYS I MAKE. SEEMS TO HAVE A LOT OF NEPHEWS AND NIECES!
OH — WOULD THAT BE THE MAN AND THE BOY WE MET, I WONDER? BOTH TALL, AND WELL BUILT — AND THE MAN HAD SHAGGY EYEBROWS.
THAT'S RIGHT. MR. CURTON AND HIS SON. THEY CAME HERE SOME WEEKS AGO. YOU OUGHT TO GET TO KNOW THE SON, JULIAN. HE'S ABOUT YOUR AGE.
DOESN'T HE GO TO ANY SCHOOL?
NO. HE'S BEEN ILL, SO HIS FATHER SAID. GOT TO HAVE PLENTY OF SEA-AIR AND THAT SORT OF THING. NOT A BAD SORT OF BOY. COMES AND HELPS ME SOMETIMES, AND HE LIKES TO MESS ABOUT WITH MY TELESCOPE.
I DO TOO. CAN I LOOK THROUGH IT NOW? I'D LIKE TO SEE IF I CAN SPOT KIRRIN ISLAND.
WELL, YOU WON'T SEE MUCH THIS WEATHER. BUT IT'LL CLEAR IN A FEW MINUTES — SEE THAT BREAK IN THE CLOUDS?
YES, YOU'LL BE ABLE TO SEE YOUR ISLAND SOON. THAT'S A FUNNY THING YOUR FATHER'S BUILT THERE, MISS. PART OF HIS WORK, I SUPPOSE.
THAT'S RIGHT. IT'S — OH, TIMMY!
PAINT
OH, COAST GUARD, I'M SO SORRY. BAD BOY, TIMMY!
NO HARM DONE. THE YOUNG FELLOW NEXT DOOR BROUGHT THIS PAINT IN. HE WAS HELPING PAINT A DOLLS' HOUSE I MADE FOR HIS FATHER.
OH DEAR. DO YOU THINK HE'LL BE CROSS WHEN HE KNOWS TIMMY SPILT IT?
SHOULDN'T THINK SO. HE'S A QUEER BOY, THOUGH — QUIET AND A BIT SULKY. NOT A BAD BOY, BUT DOESN'T SEEM VERY FRIENDLY LIKE.
TIMMY, IF YOU DARE GO NEAR ANY MORE TINS OF PAINT YOU SHAN'T SLEEP ON MY BED TONIGHT.
THE WEATHER'S A BIT CLEARER NOW. CAN WE HAVE A SQUINT THROUGH YOUR TELESCOPE, COASTGUARD?
AND SO EVERYONE HAD A TURN AT THE TELESCOPE...
OH, I CAN SEE THE ISLAND CLEARLY. AND THERE'S A RABBIT SCAMPERING!
DON'T LET THAT DOG OF YOURS SQUINT THROUGH THE TELESCOPE THEN, OR HE'LL TRY TO GET DOWN IT AFTER THAT RABBIT!

GEORGE'S TURN...
AH YES— AND THERE'S THE TOWER FATHER HAD BUILT. I CAN SEE THE GLASS ROOM QUITE CLEARLY, AND THERE'S NOBODY IN IT. NO SIGN OF FATHER ANYWHERE.
WE'D BETTER GO NOW. WE'LL BE UP AGAIN SOMETIME, AND WE'LL COME AND SEE WHAT TOYS YOU'VE MADE. THANKS FOR LETTING US LOOK THROUGH THE TELESCOPE.
YOU'RE WELCOME! YOU'RE NOT LIKELY TO WEAR IT OUT THROUGH LOOKING! COME ALONG ANY TIME YOU WANT TO USE IT.
ON THE WAY BACK THEY MET THE COASTGUARD'S YOUNG NEIGHBOUR AGAIN...
HALLO! BEEN UP TO SEE THE COASTGUARD?
YES. NICE OLD FELLOW, ISN'T HE?
I SAY, I'M SORRY BUT MY DOG UPSET YOUR TIN OF GREEN PAINT. CAN I PAY YOU FOR IT, PLEASE?
GOODNESS, NO! I DON'T MIND. THERE WASN'T MUCH LEFT OF IT ANYWAY. THAT'S A NICE DOG OF YOURS.
YES, HE IS. BEST DOG IN THE WORLD. I'VE HAD HIM FOR YEARS, BUT HE'S STILL AS YOUNG AS EVER. DO YOU LIKE DOGS?
OH YES.
THAT'S AN INTERESTING LITTLE ISLAND. I WISH I COULD GO THERE.
IT'S MY ISLAND. MY VERY OWN.
REALLY? COULD YOU LET ME GO OVER ONE DAY THEN?
WELL— NOT JUST AT PRESENT. YOU SEE, MY FATHER'S THERE— WORKING. HE'S A SCIENTIST.
REALLY? ER— I SUPPOSE HE'S GOT A NEW EXPERIMENT ON HAND, THEN— AND THAT QUEER TOWER MUST BE SOMETHING TO DO WITH IT. WHEN WILL HIS EXPERIMENT BE FINISHED?
WHAT'S THAT TO DO WITH YOU?
THE OTHERS STARED AT DICK IN SURPRISE. HE HAD SOUNDED RATHER RUDE, AND HIS QUESTION BROUGHT A SPEEDY REPLY...
OH NOTHING! I ONLY THOUGHT THAT IF HIS WORK WILL SOON BE FINISHED, PERHAPS YOUR BROTHER WOULD TAKE ME OVER TO HIS ISLAND!
GEORGE COULDN'T HELP FEELING PLEASED. THIS BOY THOUGHT SHE WAS A BOY! AND GEORGE WAS ALWAYS GRACIOUS TO PEOPLE WHO MADE THAT MISTAKE...
OF COURSE I'LL TAKE YOU! IT SHOULDN'T BE LONG BEFORE I DO— THE EXPERIMENT IS NEARLY DONE.

All about Telescopes

George and her cousins were pleased to be able to use the coastguard's telescope to view their favourite island more closely. George could look for her father and Timmy in the glass room at the top of the tower, and Anne could even see a rabbit scampering about on Kirrin Island.

If you ever have the opportunity to look through a telescope, you too will realise what a valuable instrument it is. Viewed through a telescope, not only do tiny objects appear much larger, many are so far away that we cannot see them at all without something to help our eyes.

Coastguards depend on telescopes to do their work of helping ships in distress, just as ships' captains use them to avoid danger. They may have powerful binoculars instead, but these are really two small telescopes side by side. Telescopes are also used in surveying instruments and laboratory spectroscopes, as well as in gunsights and for other military purposes.

The most important use of telescopes, however, is undoubtedly in astronomy, for without them we would know very little about the universe.

We do not know for certain who invented the telescope. Possibly it was a spectacle-maker in Holland named Hans Lippershey. There is a story that Lippershey happened to look through two lenses, one in front of the other, and found to his surprise that the objects he viewed appeared nearer and larger. So he fitted the lenses into a tube, keeping them a similar distance apart, and consequently made the first telescope.

This was in 1608, and reports of the new invention spread rapidly to other countries. When the Italian scientist Galileo heard of it the following year, he immediately built himself a telescope. He realised the potential use of telescopes in astronomy — and he was not disappointed. By using this, and several other telescopes he constructed later, Galileo made many important astronomical discoveries, including the mountains on the moon.

At first, all telescopes were made with one lens that was concave (curved inward) and one that was convex (curved outward). In 1630 a German astronomer, Johannes Kepler, found that a better telescope could be produced by using two convex lenses instead. It meant that the object viewed appeared upside down, but because the results were clearer, this kind of telescope soon came into general use for astronomy. Telescopes of this sort are called refracting telescopes or refractors.

There is another type of telescope known as a reflecting telescope or reflector, the first of

This telescope is so huge that it is lined with catwalks to enable people to get from one part to another.

Another view of the same telescope from the top end. Compare the size of the man to the size of the telescope.

which was made by the English scientist, Sir Isaac Newton, in 1668. A reflecting telescope uses a mirror which is curved, rather than an object-glass. Most of the large telescopes used in astronomy today are reflecting telescopes. There are several reasons for this. It is not so hard to make a big perfect mirror as it is a large glass lens with no flaws or bubbles in it. It is essential for a telescope to be firmly mounted, and a mirror can be supported right across its back. A lens, on the other hand, can be supported only around the edge — otherwise the supports would get in the way of the light rays. And if a lens is too heavy, it will start to sag under its own weight.

For many years, the biggest telescope in the world was the five metre Hale reflecting telescope on Mount Palomar in the United States. The Hale telescope is so big that an observer can sit in a case inside the telescope tube. The Russians have built an even larger reflecting telescope now which they have set up in the Caucasus Mountains.

Julian and his classmates have been studying astronomy at school recently, and one day they experimented with making telescopes of their own. You may like to have a go too. They found that they could make a very simple refracting telescope by fixing two magnifying glasses in a cardboard tube. Later they were lucky enough to be able to obtain two suitable lenses — one about four centimetres and another much smaller — from an optician. They positioned them in cardboard tubes that slotted snugly into each other so that they could adjust the distance between the lenses to make the picture really sharp. Then they made a stand to keep their telescope steady. Julian and his friends were thrilled with the result. In the night sky, they were even able to make out some of the craters on the moon through the telescope.

If you want a proper astronomical telescope, you will find they are very expensive to buy. A much better investment would be a pair of binoculars which don't cost nearly so much, and have the advantage of showing a right-way-up image for ordinary viewing. Field telescopes, such as the coastguard uses, contain an extra lens to turn the image the right side up. Think how confusing it would be if the coastguard had to observe upside-down ships sailing on an upside-down sea!

Chapter 7

A little squabble

'Making friends?' he said amiably. 'That's right. My boy's pretty lonely here.'

A sound made them turn. It was the boy's father coming up. He nodded to the children. 'Making friends?' he said, amiably. 'That's right. My boy's pretty lonely here. I hope you'll come up and see us some time. Finished your conversation, son?'

'Yes,' said the boy. 'This boy here says that island is his, and he's going to take me over it when his father has finished his work there—and that won't be long.'

'And do you know the way through all those wicked rocks?' said the man. '*I* shouldn't care to try it. I was talking to the fishermen the other day, and not one of them appeared to know the way!'

This was rather astonishing. Some of the fishermen *did* know it. Then the children remembered that the men had all been forbidden to take anyone to the island while Uncle Quentin was at work there. It was clear that they had pretended not to know the way, in loyalty to their orders.

'Did you want to go to the island then?' asked Dick, suddenly.

'Oh no! But my boy here would love to go,' said the man. '*I* don't want to be seasick, bobbing up and down on those waves near the island. I'm a poor sailor. I never go on the sea if I can help it!'

'Well, we must go,' said Julian. 'We've got to do some shopping for my aunt. Good-bye!'

'Come and see us as soon as you can,' said the man. 'I've a fine television set that Martin here would like to show you. Any afternoon you like!'

'Oh thanks!' said George. She seldom saw television. 'We'll come!'

They parted, and the four children and Timmy went on down the cliff-path.

'Whatever made you sound so rude, Dick?' said George. 'The way you said "What's that to do with you?" sounded quite insulting.'

'Well—I just felt suspicious, that's all,' said Dick. 'That boy seemed to be so jolly interested in the island and in your father's work, and when it would be finished.'

'Why shouldn't he be?' demanded George. 'Everyone in the village is interested. They all know about the tower. And all the boy wanted to know was when he could go to my island—that's why he asked when Father's work would be finished. I liked him.'

'You only liked him because he was ass enough to think you were a boy,' said Dick. 'Jolly girlish-looking boy you are, that's all I can say.'

George flared up at once. 'Don't be mean! I'm *not* girlish-looking. I've far more freckles than you have, for one thing, and better eyebrows. *And* I can make my voice go deep.'

'You're just silly,' said Dick, in disgust. 'As if freckles are boyish! Girls have them just as much as boys. I don't believe that boy thought you were a boy at all. He was just sucking up to you. He must have heard how much you liked playing at being what you aren't.'

George walked up to Dick with such a furious look on her face that Julian hastily put himself in between them. 'Now, no brawls,' he said. 'You're both too old to begin slapping each other like kids in the nursery. Let me tell you, you're both behaving like babies, not like boys *or* girls!'

Anne was looking on with scared eyes. George didn't go off the deep end like this usually. And it *was* funny of Dick to have spoken so rudely to the boy on the cliff. Timmy gave a sudden little whine. His tail was down, and he looked very miserable.

'Oh George—Timmy can't *bear* you to quarrel with Dick!' said

Anne. 'Look at him! He's just miserable!'

'He didn't like that boy a bit,' said Dick. 'That was another thing I thought was funny. If Timmy doesn't like a person, *I* don't like him either.'

'Timmy doesn't *always* rush round new people,' said George. 'He didn't growl or snarl, anyway. All right, all right, Julian; I'm not going to start brawling. But I do think Dick is being silly. Making a mountain out of a molehill—just because someone was interested in Kirrin Island and Father's work, and just because Timmy didn't caper all round him. He was such a solemn sort of boy that I'm not surprised Timmy wasn't all over him. He probably knew the boy wouldn't like it. Timmy's clever like that.'

'Oh, do stop,' said Dick. 'I give in—gracefully! I may be making a fuss. Probably am. I couldn't help my feelings, though.'

Anne gave a sigh of relief. The squabble was over. She hoped it wouldn't crop up again. George had been very touchy since she had been home. If only Uncle Quentin would hurry up and finish his work, and they could all go to the island as much as they liked, things would be all right.

'I'd rather like to see that television set,' said George. 'We might go up some afternoon.'

'Right,' said Julian. 'But on the whole, I think it would be best if we steered clear of any talk about your father's work. Not that we know much. Still, we do know that once before there were people after one of his theories. The secrets of the scientists are very, very important these days, you know, George. Scientists are V I P!'

'What's V I P?' asked Anne.

'Very Important People, baby!' said Julian, with a laugh. 'What did you think it meant? Violet, Indigo, Purple? I guess those are the colours Uncle Quentin would go if he knew anyone was trying to snoop into his secrets!'

Everyone laughed, even George. She looked affectionately at Julian. He was always so sensible and good-tempered. She really would go by what he said.

The day passed swiftly. The weather cleared and the sun came out strongly. The air smelt of gorse and primroses and the salt of the sea. Lovely! They went shopping for Aunt Fanny, and stopped to talk with James, the fisher-boy.

'Your father's got the island, I see,' he said to George with a grin. 'Bad luck, Miss. You'll not be going over there so often. And nobody else will, either, so I've heard.'

'That's right,' said George. 'Nobody is allowed to go over there for some time. Did you help to take some of the stuff over, James?'

'Yes. I know the way, you see, because I've been with you,' said James. 'Well, Miss, how did you find your boat when you went across yesterday? I got her all ship-shape for you, didn't I?'

'Yes, you did, James,' said George, warmly. 'You made her look beautiful. You must come across to the island with us next time we go.'

'Thanks,' said James, his ready grin showing all his white teeth. 'Like to leave Timmy with me for a week or two? See how he wants to stay!'

George laughed. She knew James was only joking. He was very fond of Timmy, though, and Timmy adored James. He was now pushing himself hard against the fisher-boy's knees, and trying to put his nose into his brown hand. Timmy had never forgotten the time when James looked after him so well.

The evening came, and the bay was softly blue. Little white horses flecked it here and there. The four gazed across to Kirrin Island. It always looked so lovely at this time of the evening.

The glass top of the tower winked and blinked in the sun. It looked almost as if someone was signalling. But there was no one in the little glass room. As the children watched they heard a faint rumbling sound, and suddenly the top of the tower was ablaze with a curious glare.

'Look! That's what happened yesterday!' said Julian, in excitement. 'Your father's at work all right, George. I do wonder what he's doing!'

Then there came a throbbing sound, almost like the noise of an aeroplane, and once more the glass top of the tower shone and blazed, as the wires became full of some curious power.

'Weird,' said Dick. 'A bit frightening too. Where's your father at this very moment, I wonder, George. How I'd like to know!'

'I bet he's forgotten all about meals again,' said George. 'Didn't he wolf our sandwiches—he must have been starving. I wish he'd let Mother go over there and look after him.'

Her mother came in at that moment. 'Did you hear the noise?' she said. 'I suppose that was your father at work again. Oh dear, I hope he doesn't blow himself up one of these days!'

'Aunt Fanny, can I stay up till half past ten tonight?' asked Anne, hopefully. 'To see Uncle Quentin's signal, you know?'

'Aunt Fanny, can I stay up till half-past ten tonight?'

'Good gracious, no!' said her aunt. 'No one needs to stay up. I am quite capable of watching for it myself!'

'Oh Aunt Fanny! Surely I and Dick can stay up!' said Julian. 'After all, we're not in bed till ten at school.'

'Yes—but this is *half past* ten, and you wouldn't even be in bed then,' said his aunt. 'There's no reason why you shouldn't lie in bed and watch for it though, if you want to—providing you haven't fallen asleep!'

'Oh yes—I can do that,' said Julian. 'My window looks across to Kirrin Island. Six flashes with a lantern? I shall count them very carefully.'

So the four went to bed at the usual time. Anne was asleep long before half past ten, and George was so drowsy that she could not make herself get up and go into the boys' room. But Dick and Julian were both wide awake. They lay in their beds and looked out of the window. There was no moon, but the sky was clear, and the stars shone down, giving a faint light. The sea looked very black. There was no sign of Kirrin Island. It was lost in the darkness of the night.

'Almost half past ten,' said Julian, looking at his watch which had luminous hands. 'Now then, Uncle Quentin, what about it?'

Almost as if his uncle was answering him, a light shone out in the glass top of the tower. It was a clear, small light, like the light of a lantern.

Julian began to count. 'One flash.' There was a pause. 'Two flashes.' Another pause. 'Three . . . four . . . five . . . six!'

The flashes stopped. Julian snuggled down into bed. 'Well, that's that. Uncle Quentin's all right. I say, it's weird to think of him climbing that spiral stairway right to the top of the tower, in the dark of night, isn't it?—just to mess about with those wires.'

'Mmmmm,' said Dick sleepily. 'I'd rather he did it, than I! You can be a scientist if you like, Ju—but *I* don't want to climb towers in the dead of night on a lonely island. I'd like Timmy there, at least!'

Someone knocked on their door and it opened. Julian sat up at once. It was Aunt Fanny.

'Oh Julian dear—did you see the flashes? I forgot to count them. Were there six?'

'Oh yes, Aunt Fanny! I'd have rushed down to tell you if anything was wrong. Uncle's all right. Don't you worry!'

'I wish I'd told him to do an *extra* flash to tell me if he's had some of that nice soup,' said his aunt. 'Well, good night, Julian. Sleep well!'

Chapter 8

Down in the quarry

DICK, IT SEEMED, WAS TRYING TO BE FRIENDLY TO MAKE UP FOR THE DAY BEFORE...
BY THE WAY, DON'T GO NEAR TIMMY UNLESS YOU WANT TO BE BURIED IN EARTH, MARTIN. HEY, TIMMY— IS A RABBIT REALLY WORTH ALL THAT HARD WORK?
APPARENTLY IT WAS, FOR TIMMY WENT ON DIGGING FOR ALL HE WAS WORTH. THEN—
OUCH! WHAT WAS THAT?
LOOK AT THIS — A JOLLY FINE ARROW-HEAD! THANKS, TIMMY, OLD FELLOW. VERY GOOD OF YOU TO GO DIGGING FOR ME. WHAT ABOUT A HAMMER-HEAD NEXT?
JOLLY GOOD SPECIMEN. SEE HOW IT'S BEEN SHAPED, GEORGE? TO THINK THIS WAS USED THOUSANDS OF YEARS AGO TO KILL THE ENEMIES OF A CAVE-MAN!
MARTIN DIDN'T SAY MUCH, AND DICK THOUGHT HE WAS A STRANGE FELLOW — A BIT DULL AND BORING. HE WONDERED IF THEY OUGHT TO ASK HIM TO THEIR PIC-NIC. HE DIDN'T WANT TO IN THE LEAST. BUT GEORGE DID!
ARE YOU HAVING A PICNIC HERE TOO?
NO. I'VE NOT BROUGHT ANY SAND-WICHES.
WELL, WE'VE PLENTY. STAY AND HAVE SOME WITH US.
THANKS. IT'S VERY NICE OF YOU. AND WILL YOU COME AND SEE MY TELEVISION SET THIS AFTERNOON IN RETURN? I'D LIKE YOU TO.
YES, WE WILL. IT WOULD BE SOMETHING TO DO! OH, ANNE— JUST LOOK AT THOSE VIOLETS! I'VE NEVER SEEN SUCH BIG WHITE ONES BEFORE!
THE BOYS CARRIED ON SCRAPING ABOUT FOR ARROW-HEADS WHILE THE GIRLS PICKED MORE AND MORE FLOWERS — AND THEN AT HALF PAST TWELVE THEY SHARED THEIR SANDWICHES WITH MARTIN, AND HE BECAME QUITE FRIENDLY...
BEST SANDWICHES I'VE EVER TASTED. I DO LIKE THESE SARDINE ONES.
DOES YOUR MOTHER MAKE THEM FOR YOU? I WISH I HAD A MOTHER. MINE DIED AGES AGO.

THERE WAS A SYMPATHETIC SILENCE... THEN THEY OFFERED MARTIN THE BIGGEST PIECE OF CAKE!
I SAW YOUR FATHER FLASHING HIS SIGNALS LAST NIGHT.
HOW DO YOU KNOW HE WAS SIGNALLING? WHO TOLD YOU?
JULIAN GAVE DICK A NUDGE, AND GEORGE SCOWLED AT HIM. THEY DIDN'T WANT HIM GOING OFF THE DEEP END AGAIN!
NOBODY TOLD ME. I JUST SAW THE SIX FLASHES, AND I THOUGHT IT MUST BE GEORGE'S FATHER.
I SUPPOSE YOU SAW MY FATHER SIGNALLING THIS MORNING TOO. I BET SCORES OF PEOPLE SAW THE FLASHES.
HE JUST HELIOGRAPHS WITH A MIRROR AT HALF PAST TEN TO SIGNAL THAT HE'S ALL RIGHT— AND FLASHES A LANTERN AT THE SAME TIME AT NIGHT.
NOW IT WAS DICK'S TURN TO SCOWL AT GEORGE. WHY GIVE AWAY ALL THIS INFORMATION? DICK FELT SURE SHE WAS DOING IT JUST TO PAY HIM BACK FOR HIS SHARP QUESTION. HE TRIED TO CHANGE THE SUBJECT...
WHERE DO YOU GO TO SCHOOL?
I DON'T. I'VE BEEN ILL.
WELL, WHERE DID YOU GO TO SCHOOL BEFORE YOU WERE ILL?
I-I HAD A TUTOR.
OH, BAD LUCK!
THEY WERE QUIET FOR A WHILE THEN, AND THEY ALL FOUND THEMSELVES WONDERING ABOUT MARTIN. WHAT A STRANGE BOY HE WAS! DID HE HAVE TO HAVE A TUTOR BECAUSE HE WAS NO GOOD AT SCHOOL AND HAD TO BE TAUGHT AT HOME? HE CERTAINLY DIDN'T LOOK STUPID. AND GEORGE THOUGHT IT VERY ODD THAT MARTIN TOOK NO NOTICE OF TIMMY. HE'D SAID HE LIKED DOGS, AND YET HE'D NOT EVEN PATTED OLD TIM ONCE. STRANGER STILL, TIMMY HAD COMPLETELY IGNORED MARTIN, AND THAT WAS MOST UNLIKE HIM. A STRANGER USUALLY RECEIVED AT LEAST A SNIFF!
ANNE WAS JUST ABOUT TO REMARK ON TIMMY'S ODD BEHAVIOUR WHEN HE YAWNED, SHOOK HIMSELF, AND LEAPT AWAY...
HE'S GOING RABBITING AGAIN. HEY, TIM— FIND ME ANOTHER ARROW-HEAD, WILL YOU, OLD FELLOW?
LYING BACK IN THE SUN THEY ALL FELT QUITE DROWSY. SOMEWHERE BELOW THEM THEY HEARD TIMMY SCRATCHING ABOUT— AND THEN THEY BEGAN TO DOZE...
MINUTES LATER, GEORGE STIRRED...
WHERE'S TIMMY? TIMMY! OH BLOW, I SUPPOSE HE'S GONE DOWN SOME EXTRA-DEEP RABBIT HOLE. TIMMY! WHERE ARE YOU?
BUT NO TIMMY CAME. NOT EVEN AN ANSWERING BARK!

Chapter 9

George makes a discovery—

George slipped down from the rock. She peered under it. There was a large opening there, scattered with stones that Timmy had loosened in his digging.

'Surely you haven't at last found a rabbit hole big enough to go down!' said George. 'TIMMY! Where are you?'

Not a bark, not a whine came from the hole. George wriggled under the shelf of rock, and peered down the burrow. Timmy had certainly made it very big. George called up to Julian.

'Julian! Throw me down your trowel, will you?'

The trowel landed by her foot. George took it and began to make the hole bigger. It might be big enough for Timmy, but it wasn't big enough for her!

She dug hard and soon got very hot. She crawled out and looked over on to the rock to see if she could get one of the others to help her. They were all asleep.

'Lazy things!' thought George, quite forgetting that she too would have been dozing if she hadn't wondered where Timmy had gone.

She slipped down under the rock again and began to dig hard with her trowel. Soon she had made the hole big enough to get through. She was surprised to find quite a large passage, once she had made the entrance big enough to take her. She could crawl along on hands and knees!

'I say—I wonder if this is just some animal's runway—or leads somewhere!' thought George.

George took the trowel and began to make the hole bigger.

'TIMMY! Where *are* you?'

From somewhere deep in the quarry side there came a faint whine. George felt thankful. So Timmy *was* there, after all. She crawled along, and then quite suddenly the tunnel became high and wide and she realized that she must be in a passage. It was perfectly dark, so she could not see anything, she could only feel.

Then she heard the sound of pattering feet, and Timmy pressed affectionately against her legs, whining. 'Oh, Timmy—you gave me a bit of a fright!' said George. 'Where have you been? Is this a real passage—or just a tunnel in the quarry, made by the old miners, and now used by animals?'

'Woof,' said Timmy, and pulled at George's jeans to make her go back to the daylight.

'All right, I'm coming!' said George. 'Don't imagine I want to

and loses her temper

wander alone in the dark! I only came to look for you.'

She made her way back to the shelf of rock. By this time Dick was awake, and wondered where George had gone. He waited a few minutes, blinking up into the deep blue sky, and then sat up.

'George!' There was no answer. So, in his turn Dick slipped down from the rock and looked around. And, to his very great astonishment he saw first Timmy, and then George on hands and knees, appearing out of the hole under the rock. He stared open-mouthed, and George began to giggle.

'It's all right. I've only been rabbiting with Timmy!'

She stood beside him, shaking and brushing soil from her jersey and trousers. 'There's a passage behind the entrance to the hole under the rock,' she said. 'At first it's just a narrow tunnel, like an animal's hole—then it gets wider—and then it becomes a proper high wide passage! I couldn't see if it went on, of course, because it was dark. Timmy was a long way in.'

'Good gracious!' said Dick. 'It sounds exciting.'

'Let's explore it, shall we?' said George. 'I expect Julian's got a torch.'

'No,' said Dick. 'We won't explore today.'

The others were now awake, and listening with interest. 'Is it a secret passage?' said Anne, thrilled. 'Oh do let's explore it!'

'No, not today,' said Dick again. He looked at Julian. Julian guessed that Dick did not want Martin to share this secret. Why should he? He was not a real friend of theirs, and they had only just got to know him. He nodded back at Dick.

'No, we won't explore today. Anyway, it may be nothing—just an old tunnel made by the quarrymen.'

Martin was listening with great interest. He went and looked into the hole. 'I wish we could explore,' he said. 'Maybe we could plan to meet again with torches and see if there really is a passage there.'

Julian looked at his watch. 'Nearly two o'clock. Well, Martin, if we're going to see that half past two programme of yours, we'd better be getting on.'

Carrying baskets of primroses and violets, the girls began to climb up the steep side of the quarry. Julian took Anne's basket from her, afraid she might slip and fall. Soon they were all at the top. The air felt quite cool there after the warmth of the quarry.

They made their way to the cliff path and before long were passing the coastguard's cottage. He was out in his garden, and he waved to them.

They went in the gateway of the next-door cottage. Martin pushed the door open. His father was sitting at the window of the room inside, reading. He got up with a broad, welcoming smile.

'Well, well, well! This *is* nice! Come along in, do. Yes, the dog as well. I don't mind dogs a bit. I like them.'

It seemed rather a crowd in the small room. They all shook hands politely. Martin explained hurriedly that he had brought the children to see a television programme.

'A good idea,' said Mr Curton, still beaming. Anne stared at his great eyebrows. They were very long and thick. She wondered why he didn't have them trimmed—but perhaps he liked them like that. They made him look very fierce, she thought.

The four looked round the little room. There was a television set standing at the far end, on a table. There was also a magnificent wireless—and something else that made the boys stare with interest.

'Hallo! You've got a transmitting set, as well as a receiving set,' said Julian.

They began to climb up the steep side of the quarry.

'Yes,' said Mr Curton. 'It's a hobby of mine. I made that set.'

'Yes,' said Mr Curton. 'It's a hobby of mine. I made that set.'

'Well! You must be brainy!' said Dick.

'What's a transmitting set?' asked Anne. 'I haven't heard of one before.'

'Oh, it just means a set to send out messages by wireless—like police-cars have, when they send back messages to the police stations,' said Dick. 'This is a very powerful one, though.'

Martin was fiddling about with the television switches. Then the programme began.

It was great fun seeing the television programme. When it was over Mr Curton asked them to stay to tea.

'Now don't say no,' he said. 'I'll ring up and ask your aunt, if you like, if you're afraid she might be worried.'

'Well—if you'd do that, sir,' said Julian. 'I think she *would* wonder where we'd gone!'

Mr Curton rang up Aunt Fanny. Yes, it was quite all right for them to stay, but they mustn't be too late back. So they settled down to an unexpectedly good tea. Martin was not very talkative, but Mr Curton made up for it. He laughed and joked and was altogether very good company.

The talk came round to Kirrin Island. Mr Curton said how beautiful it looked each evening. George looked pleased.

'Yes,' she said. '*I* always think that. I do wish Father hadn't chosen this particular time to work on my island. I'd planned to go and stay there.'

'I suppose you know every inch of it!' said Mr Curton.

'Oh yes!' said George. 'We all do. There are dungeons there, you know—real dungeons that go deep down—where we once found some gold ingots.'

'Yes—I remember reading about that,' said Mr Curton. 'That must have been exciting. Fancy *finding* the dungeons too! And there's an old well too you once got down, isn't there?'

'Yes,' said Anne, remembering. 'And there is a cave where we once lived—it's got an entrance through the roof, as well as from the sea.'

'And I suppose your father is conducting his marvellous experiments down in the dungeons?' said Mr Curton. 'Well, what a strange place to work in!'

'No—we don't . . .' began George, when she got a kick on the ankle from Dick. She screwed up her face in pain. It had been a very sharp kick indeed.

'What were you going to say?' said Mr Curton, looking surprised.

'Er—I was just going to say that—er—er—we don't know which place Father has chosen,' said

George, keeping her legs well out of the way of Dick's feet.

Timmy gave a sudden sharp whine. George looked down at him in surprise. He was looking up at Dick, with a very hurt expression.

'What's the matter, Timmy!' said George anxiously.

'He's finding the room too hot, I think,' said Dick. 'Better take him out, George.'

George feeling quite anxious, took him out. Dick joined her. She scowled at him. 'What did you want to kick me for like that? I shall have a frightful bruise.'

'You know jolly well why I did,' said Dick. 'Giving away everything like that! Can't you see the chap's very interested in your father being on the island? There may be nothing in it at all, but you might at least keep your mouth shut. Just like a girl, can't help blabbing. I had to stop you somehow. I don't mind telling you I trod jolly hard on poor old Timmy's tail too, to make him yelp, so that you'd stop talking!'

'Oh—you beast!' said George, indignantly. 'How *could* you hurt Timmy.

'I didn't want to. It was a shame,' said Dick, stopping to fondle Timmy's ears. 'Poor old Tim. I didn't want to hurt you, old fellow.'

'I'm going home,' said George, her face scarlet with anger. 'I hate you for talking to me like that—telling me I blab like a girl—and stamping on poor Timmy's tail. You can go back and say I'm taking Timmy home.'

'Right,' said Dick. 'And a jolly good thing too. The less you talk to Mr Curton the better. *I'm* going back to find out exactly what he is and what he does. I'm getting jolly suspicious. You'd better go before you give anything else away!'

Almost choking with rage, George went off with Timmy. Dick went back to make her apologies. Julian and Anne, sure that something was up, felt most uncomfortable. They rose to go, but to their surprise, Dick became very talkative and appeared to be suddenly very much interested in Mr Curton and what he did.

But at last they said good-bye and went. 'Come again, do,' said Mr Curton, beaming at the three of them. 'And tell the other boy—what's his name, George—that I hope his dog is quite all right again now. Such a nice, well-behaved dog! Well good-bye! We'll see you again soon, I hope!'

Almost choking with rage, George went off with Timmy.

'What did you want to kick me for like that?'

General Knowledge Crossword

A favourite indoor pastime of the Five is solving crossword puzzles. Test your brain power and see how quickly you can do this crossword.

Clues Across

1. Large African antelope (3)
3. Home for pigs (3)
5. Tree, which grows clusters of berries (5)
6. Slightly wet (4)
7. A hot drink (3)
9. Type of tree (3)
11. Cannot find your way (4)
13. Norse god of thunder (4)
15. Not down (2)
17. _____ and Juliet (5)
19. Breed of dog (7)
20. Plants will grow from this (4)

Clues Down

1. Opposite of 'stop' (2)
2. One of a European mountain range (3)
3. The sun will do this (3)
4. English river (5)
5. Australian bird (3)
6. To run quickly (4)
8. French cathedral city (5)
9. The smallest particle from which anything is made (4)
10. Domestic animal (5)
12. To ruin something (5)
14. You can tie knots in this (4)
16. You can draw water from this (4)
18. Insane (3)

Answers on page 90.

Chapter 10

A surprising signal

THAT EVENING JULIAN, DICK AND ANNE PLAYED MONOPOLY UNTIL IT WAS TIME FOR BED. JULIAN STAYED AWAKE TO WATCH FOR HIS UNCLE'S SIGNAL— SIX FLASHES— WHICH CAME AT EXACTLY HALF PAST TEN. HE SOON FELL ASLEEP, BUT WAS AWAKENED LATER BY A STRANGE THROBBING SOUND. HE SAT UP, EXPECTING TO SEE THE TOP OF THE TOWER ABLAZE WITH LIGHT, AS IT SOMETIMES WAS WHEN HIS UNCLE CONDUCTED A SPECIAL EXPERIMENT. BUT NOTHING HAPPENED, AND SOON THE THROBBING DIED AWAY...

NEXT MORNING...
I SAW UNCLE'S SIGNALS ALL RIGHT LAST NIGHT, AUNT FANNY. DID YOU?
YES. JULIAN, DO YOU THINK YOU WOULD WATCH FOR THEM THIS MORNING, DEAR? I HAVE TO GO TO THE VICARAGE.
YES, OF COURSE I WILL, AUNT FANNY. I'LL WRITE SOME LETTERS SITTING BY THE WINDOW IN MY ROOM — AND AT HALF PAST TEN I'LL WATCH FOR THE SIGNALS.
THE LETTER-WRITING SESSION WAS INTERRUPTED BY EACH OF THE OTHERS IN TURN, INCLUDING GEORGE WHO WAS TRYING TO BE SPECIALLY NICE TO MAKE UP FOR YESTERDAY'S TEMPER!
COMING FOR A GAME ON THE BEACH, JU?
I'LL COME AT HALF PAST TEN, AFTER I'VE SEEN THE SIGNALS FROM THE TOWER. THEY'RE DUE IN TEN MINUTES.
THE SIGNAL CAME EXACTLY ON TIME...
ONE FLASH— TWO—THREE—FOUR— FIVE—SIX. HE'S ALL RIGHT.
BUT JUST AS JULIAN WAS ABOUT TO TURN AWAY...
ANOTHER FLASH—SEVEN! AND ANOTHER! EIGHT—NINE—TEN—ELEVEN—TWELVE! HOW QUEER. WHY TWELVE FLASHES? HALLO, HERE WE GO AGAIN!
ANOTHER SIX FLASHES CAME FROM THE TOWER—AND A MINUTE OR TWO LATER JULIAN HEARD THE OTHERS POUNDING UP THE STAIRS...
JULIAN! FATHER FLASHED EIGHTEEN TIMES INSTEAD OF SIX! DO YOU THINK HE COULD BE IN SOME SORT OF TROUBLE?
I SHOULDN'T THINK SO. IF HE WAS HE'D FLASH THE S.O.S. SIGNAL.
HE DOESN'T KNOW MORSE!
WELL, I EXPECT HE JUST WANTS TO LET US KNOW THAT HE NEEDS SOME-THING. MORE FOOD, PERHAPS.
SO, WHEN AUNT FANNY CAME HOME THEY SUGGESTED THEY SHOULD ALL GO OVER TO THE ISLAND...
OH YES! THAT WOULD BE NICE. I EXPECT YOUR UNCLE WANTS A MESSAGE SENT OFF SOME-WHERE. GEORGE, YOU'D BETTER RUN DOWN AND TELL JAMES YOU'LL BE WANTING THE BOAT.
LATER THAT MORNING, AS THEY ROUNDED THE LOW WALL OF ROCKS AND CAME INTO THE LITTLE COVE, UNCLE QUENTIN WAS WAITING FOR THEM...
WE SAW YOUR TREBLE SIGNAL. DID YOU WANT SOMETHING, DEAR?
YES, I DID. WHAT'S THAT YOU'VE GOT IN YOUR BASKET, FANNY? MORE OF THOSE DELI-CIOUS SANDWICHES?

OH, QUENTIN— HAVEN'T YOU BEEN HAVING PROPER MEALS AGAIN? WHAT ABOUT THAT LOVELY SOUP?
WHAT SOUP? I WISH I'D KNOWN ABOUT IT. I COULD HAVE DONE WITH SOME LAST NIGHT.
BUT QUENTIN! I TOLD YOU ABOUT IT BEFORE. IT WILL BE BAD BY NOW. YOU MUST POUR IT AWAY. WHERE IS IT? PERHAPS I'D BETTER POUR IT AWAY MYSELF.
NO. I'LL DO IT. LET'S SIT DOWN AND HAVE OUR LUNCH.
AUNT FANNY THOUGHT IT WAS MUCH TOO EARLY FOR LUNCH, BUT THE CHILDREN WERE ALWAYS READY FOR A MEAL! AND UNCLE QUENTIN DEVOURED SANDWICH AFTER SANDWICH!
WELL, DEAR— HOW IS YOUR WORK GETTING ON?
OH, VERY WELL INDEED. COULDN'T BE BETTER. JUST GOT TO A MOST TRICKY AND INTERESTING STAGE.
WHY DID YOU SIGNAL EIGHTEEN TIMES, UNCLE QUENTIN?
AH, WELL— IT'S DIFFICULT TO EXPLAIN, REALLY. THE FACT IS— I CAN'T HELP FEELING THERE'S SOMEBODY ELSE ON THIS ISLAND BESIDES MYSELF
QUENTIN! WHAT IN THE WORLD DO YOU MEAN?
A LITTLE SHIVER SHOT DOWN ANNE'S SPINE...
OH DON'T UNCLE! IT SOUNDS HORRID. AND YOU'RE ALL ALONE AT NIGHT TOO!
AH, THAT'S JUST IT! I WOULDN'T MIND IF I WAS ALL ALONE AT NIGHT... WHAT WORRIES ME IS THAT I DON'T THINK I SHALL BE ALL ALONE!
YOU SEE, LATE LAST NIGHT— ABOUT HALF PAST THREE THIS MORNING— I'D JUST FINISHED AN EXPERIMENT AND CAME OUT INTO THE OPEN FOR A BREATH OF FRESH AIR... AND I COULD SWEAR I HEARD SOMEBODY COUGH. YES, COUGH TWICE.
BUT QUENTIN— YOU MIGHT HAVE IMAGINED IT!
UNCLE QUENTIN REACHED INTO HIS POCKET...
YES, I KNOW— BUT I COULDN'T IMAGINE THIS, COULD I?
A CIGARETTE END! QUITE RECENTLY DISCARDED BY THE LOOK OF IT.
NOW, I DON'T SMOKE. NOR DO ANY OF YOU. SO WHO SMOKED THIS CIGARETTE? AND HOW DID HE COME HERE? NO ONE WOULD BRING HIM BY BOAT— AND THAT'S THE ONLY WAY HERE.
A SILENCE FELL OVER THEM AS THE MYSTERY PLAYED GAMES WITH THEIR IMAGINATION. THEN AT LAST AUNT FANNY SPOKE...
WELL, QUENTIN— WHAT ARE YOU GOING TO DO?
I'LL BE ALL RIGHT IF GEORGE WILL GIVE HER CONSENT TO SOMETHING. I WANT TIMMY HERE, GEORGE! WILL YOU LEAVE HIM BEHIND WITH ME?

Chapter 11

George makes a hard choice

'But, Father–Timmy and I have never been separated once.'

There was a horrified silence. George stared at her father in complete dismay. Everyone waited to see what she would say.

'But, Father—Timmy and I have never been separated once,' she said at last, in a pleading voice. 'I do see you want him to guard you—and you *can* have him—but I'll have to stay here too!'

'Oh no!' said her father at once. 'You can't possibly stay, George. That's out of the question. As for never being separated from Timmy, well surely you wouldn't mind that for once? If it was to ensure my safety?'

George swallowed hard. This was the most difficult decision she had ever had to make in her life. Leave Timmy behind on the island—where there was some unknown hidden enemy, likely to harm him if he possibly could!

And yet there was father too—he might be in danger if there was no one to guard him.

'I shall just *have* to stay here, Father,' she said. 'I can't leave Timmy behind unless I stay too. It's no good.'

Her father began to lose his temper. He was like George—he wanted his own way, and if he didn't have it he was going to make a fuss!

'If I'd asked Julian or Dick or Anne this same thing, and they'd had a dog, they would all have said yes, at once!' he raged. 'But you, George, you must always make things difficult if you can! You and that dog—anyone would think he was worth a thousand pounds!'

'He's worth much more than that to me,' said George, in a trembling voice. Timmy crept nearer to her and pushed his nose into her hand. She held his collar as if she would not let him go for a moment.

'Yes. That dog's worth more to you than your father or mother or anyone,' said her father, in disgust.

'No, Quentin, I can't have you saying things like that,' said his wife, firmly. 'That's just silly. A mother and father are quite different from a dog—they're loved in different ways. But you are perfectly right, of course—Timmy *must* stay behind with you—and I shall certainly not allow George to stay with him. I'm not going to have *both* of you exposed to danger. It's bad enough to worry about *you*, as it is.'

George looked at her mother in dismay.

'Mother! Do tell Father I must stay here with Timmy.'

'Certainly not,' said her mother. 'Now, George, be unselfish. If it were left to Tim to decide, you know perfectly well that he would stay here—and stay *without* you. He would say to himself, "I'm needed here—my eyes are needed to spy out enemies, my ears to hear a quiet footfall—and maybe my teeth to protect my master. I shall be parted from George for a few days—but she, like me, is big enough to put up with that!" That's what Timmy would say, George, if it were left to him.'

Everyone had been listening to this unexpected speech with great attention. It was about the only one that could persuade George to give in willingly!

She looked at Timmy. He looked back at her, wagging his tail. Then he did an extraordinary thing—he got up, walked over to George's father, and lay down beside him, looking at George as if to say 'There you are! Now you know what *I* think is right!'

'You see?' said her mother. 'He agrees with me. You've always said that Timmy was a good dog, and this proves it. He knows what his duty is. You ought to be proud of him.'

'I am,' said George, in a choky voice. She got up and walked off. 'All right,' she said over her shoulder. 'I'll leave him on the island with Father. I'll come back in a minute.'

Anne got up to go after poor George, but Julian pulled her down again. 'Leave her alone! She'll be all right. Good old Timmy—you know what's right and what's wrong, don't you? Good dog, splendid dog!'

Timmy wagged his tail. He did not attempt to follow George. No—he meant to stay by her father now, even though he would much rather be with his mistress. He was sorry that George was unhappy—but sometimes it was better to do a hard thing and be unhappy about it, than try to be happy without doing it.

'Oh, Quentin dear, I don't like this business of you being here and somebody else spying on you,' said his wife, 'I really don't. How long will you be before you've finished your work?'

'A few days more,' said her husband. He looked at Timmy admiringly. 'That dog might almost have known what you were saying, Fanny, just now. It was remarkable the way he walked straight over to me.'

'He's a very clever dog,' said Anne warmly. 'Aren't you, Tim? You'll be quite safe with him, Uncle Quentin. He's terribly fierce when he wants to be!'

'Yes. I shouldn't care to have him leaping at *my* throat,' said her uncle. 'He's so big and powerful. Are there any more pieces of cake?'

'Quentin, it's really too bad of you to go without your meals,' said his wife. 'It's no good telling me you haven't, because you wouldn't be as ravenous as this if you had had your food regularly.'

'I'm leaving Timmy behind for you—but please will you do something for me?'

Her husband took no notice of what she was saying. He was looking up at his tower. 'Do you ever see those wires at the top blaze out?' he asked. 'Wonderful sight, isn't it?'

'Uncle, you're not inventing a new atom bomb, or anything are you?' asked Anne.

Her uncle looked at her scornfully. 'I wouldn't waste my time inventing things that will be used to kill and maim people! No—I'm inventing something that will be of the greatest use to mankind. You wait and see!'

George came back. 'Father,' she said, 'I'm leaving Timmy behind for you—but please will you do something for me?'

'What?' asked her father. 'No silly conditions now! I shall feed Timmy regularly, and look after him, if that's what you want to ask me. I may forget my own meals, but you ought to know me well enough to know I shouldn't neglect any animal dependent on me.'

'Yes—I know, Father,' said George, looking a bit doubtful all the same. 'What I wanted to ask you was this—when you go up in the tower to signal each morning, will you please take Timmy with you? I shall be up at the coastguard's cottage, looking through his telescope at the glass room in the tower—and I shall be able to see Timmy then. If I catch just a glimpse of him each day and know he's all right, I shan't worry so much.'

'Very well,' said her father. 'But I don't suppose for a moment that Timmy will be able to climb up the spiral stairway.'

'Oh, he can, Father—he's been up it once already,' said George.

'Good heavens!' said her father. 'Has the dog been up there too? All right, George—I promise I'll take him up with me each morning that I signal, and get him to wag his tail at you. There! Will that satisfy you?'

'Yes. Thank you,' said George. 'And you'll give him a few kind words and a pat occasionally, Father, won't you . . . and. . . ?'

'And put his bib on for him at meal-times, I suppose, and clean his teeth for him at night!' said her father, looking cross again. 'I shall treat Timmy like a proper grown-up dog, a friend of mine, George—and believe me, that's the way he wants me to treat him. Isn't it, Timmy? You like all those frills to be kept for your mistress, don't you, not for me?'

'Woof,' said Timmy, and thumped his tail. The children looked at him admiringly. He really was a very sensible clever dog. He seemed somehow much more grown-up than George.

'Uncle, if anything goes wrong, or you want help or anything, flash eighteen times again,' said Julian. 'You ought to be all right with Timmy. He's better than a dozen policemen—but you never know.'

'Right. Eighteen flashes if I want you over here for anything,' said his uncle. 'I'll remember. Now you'd better all go. It's time I got on with my work.'

'You'll pour that soup away, won't you, Quentin?' said his wife, anxiously. 'You don't want to make yourself ill by eating bad soup. It must be green by now! It would be so like you to forget all about it while it was fresh and good—and only remember when it was bad!'

'What a thing to say!' said her husband, getting up. 'Anyone would think I was five years old, without a brain in my head, the way you talk to me!'

'You've plenty of brains, dear, we all know that,' said his wife. 'But you don't seem very old sometimes! Now look after yourself—and keep Timmy by you all the time.'

'Father won't need to bother about *that*,' said George. 'Timmy will keep by *him*! You're on guard, Timmy, aren't you? And you know what *that* means!'

'Woof,' said Timmy, solemnly. He went with them all to the boat, but

Timmy stood by George's father and watched the boat bob away over the water.

he did not attempt to get in. He stood by George's father and watched the boat bob away over the water. 'Good-bye, Timmy!' shouted George, in a funny fierce voice. 'Look after yourself!'

Her father waved, and Timmy wagged his tail. George took one of the pairs of oars from Dick and began to row furiously, her face red with the hard work.

Julian looked at her in amusement. It was hard work for him, too, to keep up with the furious rowing, but he didn't say anything. He knew all this fury in rowing was George's way of hiding her grief at parting with Timmy. Funny old George! She was always so intense about things—furiously happy or furiously unhappy, in the seventh heaven of delight or down in the very depths of despair or anger.

Everyone talked hard so that George would think they were not noticing her feelings at parting with Timmy. The talk, of course, was mostly about the unknown man on the island. It seemed very mysterious indeed that he should suddenly have arrived.

'How did he get there? I'm sure not one of the fishermen would have taken him,' said Dick. 'He must have gone at night, of course, and I doubt if there is anyone but George who would know the way in the dark—or even dare to try and find it. These rocks are so close together, and so near the surface; one yard out of the right course and any boat would have a hole in the bottom!'

'No one could reach the island by swimming from the shore,' said Anne. 'It's too far, and the sea is too rough over these rocks. I honestly do wonder if there *is* anyone on the island after all. Perhaps that cigarette end was an old one.'

'It didn't look it,' said Julian. 'Well, it just beats me how anyone got there?'

He fell into thought, puzzling out all the possible and impossible ways. Then he gave an exclamation. The others looked at him.

'I've just thought—would it be possible for an aeroplane to parachute anyone down on the island? I did hear a throbbing noise one night—was it last night? It must have been a plane's engine, of course! *Could* anyone be dropped on the island?'

'Easily,' said Dick. 'I believe you've hit on the explanation, Ju! Good for you! But I say—whoever it is must be in deadly earnest, to risk being dropped on a small island like that in the dark of night!'

In deadly earnest! That didn't sound at all nice. A little shiver went down Anne's back. 'I *am* glad Timmy's there with Uncle Quentin,' she said. And everyone felt the same—yes even George!

Speeding the Message

All down the centuries people have had lots of ideas for speeding messages over long distances. There have been runners, native drums, beacon fires and smoke signals. Carrier pigeons have done a good job in times of war, and today, of course, radio waves are the fastest message carriers, moving at the speed of light, 186,000 miles a second!

Uncle Quentin, you will remember, used the heliograph idea for flashing his daily messages from the tower on Kirrin Island. The heliograph is an instrument once much used by armies and navies for transmitting messages over considerable distances. The signals are made by a movable mirror to reflect the sun's rays, or artificial light. In this method of signalling, long and short flashes in the Morse code are used. The heliograph was much used in the South African War in 1899–1902.

Julian and the rest of the Five (Timmy excepted!) all knew the Morse code. The code is known and used the world over and enables messages to be sent by flag, lamp, telegraph and radio. The man who gave us 'flying words' was Samuel Morse, an American who gave up a successful career as an artist to work on inventing the electric telegraph.

The code uses a system of dots and dashes (or short and long light signals) to make letters and words and is quite easy to learn.

Samuel Morse's problem was how to send his code of dots and dashes electrically along wires for long distances. He worked on the problem for many years, and finally succeeded in perfecting his instrument in 1837. Much to his disappointment no-one showed any great interest in his invention.

It was not until 1843 that the United States Congress voted enough money for Morse to build a line from Washington to Baltimore, a distance of 34 miles. The very first message, 'What hath God wrought', was sent the following year. It created a great sensation and before long the electric telegraph and Morse code began spreading around the world.

If you are a Scout or a Guide you will probably already know how to pass messages by means of the semaphore code. By holding your arms in certain positions you can signal all the letters of the alphabet. If you hold a flag (or even a large white handkerchief) in each hand you can have great fun signalling messages from hilltops or across fields and valleys.

In times of emergency, knowledge of one or other of the signalling codes could prove extremely useful. It could even be the means of saving your own, or other people's lives. Messages sent by Morse, heliograph or semaphore have saved the lives of countless thousands of people in distress.

If you don't know any of the codes at the moment, start mastering one today. If you can only manage 'S.O.S.' it will be time well spent.

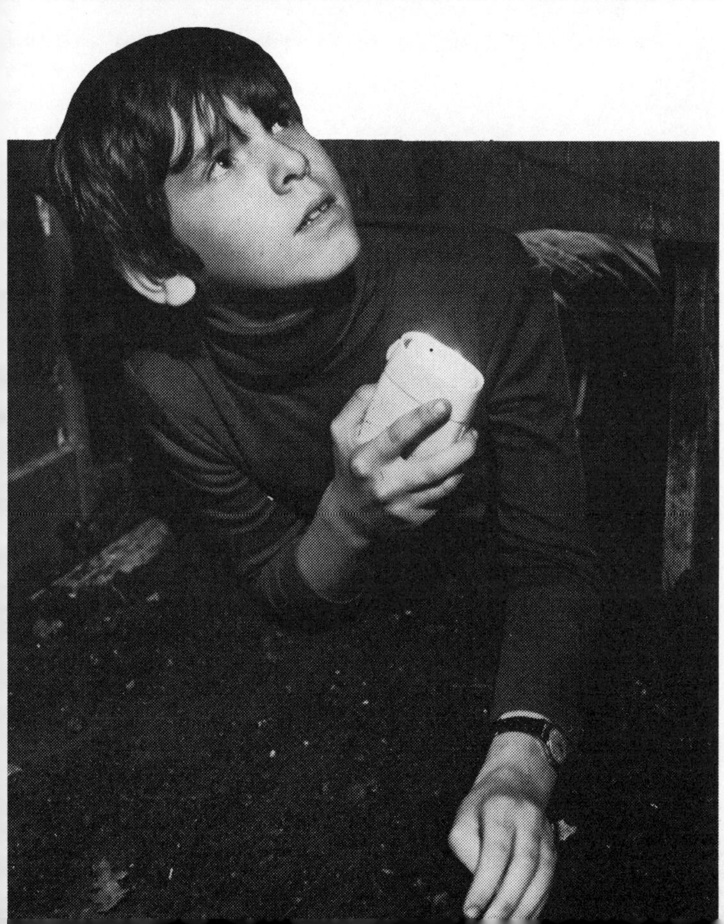

Dick demonstrates the advantages of having a torch in an emergency. Here he is using his knowledge of morse code to signal for help.

Island Quiz

After visiting Kirrin Island the Five became interested in other islands. Test your knowledge against theirs in this quiz.

1. On what island did Baden-Powell hold his first Scout camp?
2. How many islands are there in the Scilly Isles group?
3. Which are the four largest islands in the Channel Islands group?
4. What famous tweed is made on a Scottish isle?
5. Which is the most remote island in the world?
6. Which island in Britain has its own government?
7. This island is famous for its huge figures of carved stone.
8. On which island would you find a Lake of Pitch?
9. This group of islands is famous for its flower-growing.
10. On which Scottish island did St. Columba land?
11. Name the island off the Welsh coast where monks make perfumes.
12. This island is famous for making rum.
13. Island off the English coast where Queen Victoria had a large house.
14. Name the world's largest island. (Australia is not classed as an island.)
15. Is Gibraltar an island?
16. Real dragons survive on this island.
17. For what purpose was Devil's Island, in the Pacific, used?
18. This island is often called the 'Emerald Isle'.
19. Napoleon was held prisoner on this island.
20. Name the island said to have inspired the story of Robinson Crusoe.

Answers on page 90.

Chapter 12

The old map again

It was only about half past one when they arrived back, because they had had lunch so very early, and had not stayed long on the island. Joanna was most surprised to see them.

'Well, here you are again!' she said. 'I hope you don't all want another lunch, because there's nothing in the house till I go to the butcher's!'

'Oh no, Joanna—we've had our picnic lunch,' said her mistress, 'and it was a good thing we packed so much, because the master ate quite half of the lunch! He still hasn't had that nice soup we made for him. Now it will be bad of course.'

'Oh, the men! They're as bad as children!' said Joanna.

'*Well!*' said George. 'Do you really think any of *us* would let your good soup go bad, Joanna? You know jolly well we'd probably eat it up before we ought to!'

'That's true—I wouldn't accuse any of you four—or Timmy either —of playing about with your food,' said Joanna. 'You make good work of it, the lot of you. But where is Timmy?'

'I left him behind to look after Father,' said George. Joanna stared at her in surprise. She knew how passionately fond of Timmy George was.

'You're a very good girl—sometimes!' she said. 'See now—if you're still hungry because your father has eaten most of your lunch, you go and look in the biscuit tin. I made you some of your favourite ginger biscuits this morning. You go and find them.'

That was always Joanna's way! If she thought anyone was upset, she offered them her best and freshest food. George went off to find the biscuits.

'You're a kind soul, Joanna,' said George's mother. 'I'm so thankful we left Timmy there. I feel happier about the master now.'

'What shall we do this afternoon?' said Dick, when they had finished munching the delicious ginger biscuits. 'I say, aren't these good? You know, I do think good cooks deserve some kind of decoration, just as much as good soldiers or scientists, or writers. I should give Joanna the OBCBE.'

'Whatever's that?' said Julian.

'Order of the Best Cooks of the British Empire,' said Dick grinning. 'What did you think it was? "Oh, Be Careful Before Eating"?'

'You're a very good girl—sometimes!'

George disappeared upstairs and came down again with the map. It was made of thick parchment, and was yellow with age.

'You really are an absolute donkey,' said Julian. 'Now, what *shall* we do this afternoon?'

'Go and explore the passage in the quarry,' said George.

Julian cocked an eye at the window. 'It's about to pour with rain,' he said. 'I don't think that clambering up and down the steep sides of that quarry in the wet would be very easy. No—we'll leave that till a fine day.'

'I'll tell you what we'll do,' said Anne suddenly. 'Do you remember that old map of Kirrin Castle we once found in a box? It had plans of the castle in it—a plan of the dungeons, and of the ground floor, and of the top part. Well, let's have it out and study it? Now we know there is another hiding-place somewhere, we might be able to trace it on that old map. It's sure to be on it somewhere—but perhaps we didn't notice it before!'

The others looked at her, thrilled. 'Now that really is a brilliant idea of yours, Anne,' said Julian, and Anne glowed with pleasure at his praise. 'A very fine idea indeed. Just the thing for a wet afternoon. Where's the map? I suppose you've got it somewhere safe, George?'

'Oh yes,' said George. 'It's still in that old wooden box, inside the tin lining. I'll get it.'

She disappeared upstairs and came down again with the map. It was made of thick parchment, and was yellow with age. She laid it out on the table. The others bent over it, eager to look at it once more.

'Do you remember how frightfully excited we were when we first found the box?' said Dick.

'Yes, and we couldn't open it, so we threw it out of the top window down to the ground below, hoping it would burst open!' said George.

'And the crash woke up Uncle Quentin,' said Anne, with a giggle. 'And he came out and got the box and wouldn't let us have it!'

'Oh dear yes—and poor Julian had to wait till Uncle Quentin was asleep, and creep in and get the box to see what was in it!' finished Dick. 'And we found this map—and how we pored over it!'

They all pored over it again. It was in three parts, as Anne had said—a plan of the dungeons, a plan of the ground floor and a plan of the top part.

'It's no good bothering about the top part of the castle,' said Dick. 'It's all fallen down and ruined. There's practically none of it left except for that one tower.'

'I say!' said Julian, suddenly putting his finger on a certain spot in

They all pored over the map again.

the map, 'do you remember there were *two* entrances to the dungeons? One that seemed to start somewhere about that little stone room—and the other that started where we did at last find the entrance? Well—we never found the other entrance, did we?'

'No! We didn't!' said George, in excitement. She pushed Julian's finger away from the map. 'Look—there are steps shown here—somewhere where that little room is—so there *must* be an entrance there! Here's the *other* flight of steps—the ones we did find, near the well.'

'I remember that we hunted pretty hard for the entrance in the little room,' said Dick. 'We scraped away the weeds from every single stone, and gave it up at last. Then we found the other entrance, and forgot all about this one.'

'And *I* think Father has found the entrance we *didn't* find!' said George, triumphantly. 'It leads underground, obviously. Whether or not it joins up with the dungeons we know I can't make out from this map. It's a bit blurred here. But it's quite plain that there *is* an entrance here, with stone steps leading underground somewhere! See, there's some sort of passage or tunnel marked, leading from the steps. Goodness knows where it goes, it's so smeared.'

'It joins up with the dungeons, I expect,' said Julian. 'We never explored the whole of them, you know—they're so vast and weird. If we explored the whole place, we should probably come across the stone steps leading from somewhere near that little room. Still, they may be ruined or fallen in now.'

'No, they can't be,' said George. 'I'm perfectly *sure* that's the entrance Father has found. And I'll tell you something that seems to prove it, too.'

'What?' said everyone.

'Well, do you remember the other day when we first went to see Father?' said George. 'He didn't let us stay long, and he came to see us off at the boat. Well, we tried to see where he went, but we couldn't—but Dick said he saw the jackdaws rising up in a flock, as if they had been suddenly disturbed—and he wondered if Father had gone somewhere in that direction.'

Julian whistled. 'Yes—the jackdaws build in the tower, which is by the little room—and anyone going into the room would disturb them. I believe you're right, George.'

'It's been puzzling me awfully where Uncle Quentin could be doing his work,' said Dick. 'I simply could *not* solve the mystery—but now I think we have!'

'I wonder how Father found his hiding-place,' said George, thoughtfully. 'I still think it was mean of him not to tell me.'

'There must have been some reason,' said Dick, sensibly. 'Don't start brooding again!'

'I'm not,' said George. 'I'm puzzled, that's all. I wish we could take the boat and go over to the island at once, and explore!'

'Yes. I bet we'd find the entrance all right now,' said Dick. 'Your father is sure to have left some trace of where it is—a stone a bit cleaner than the rest—or weeds scraped off—or something.'

'Do you suppose the unknown enemy on the island knows Uncle Quentin's hiding-place?' said Anne, suddenly. 'Oh, I do hope he doesn't! He could so easily shut him in if he did.'

'Well, he hasn't gone there to shut Uncle up—he's gone there to steal his secret, or find it out,' said Julian. 'Golly, I'm thankful he's got Timmy. Timmy could tackle a dozen enemies.'

'Not if they had guns,' said George, in a small voice. There was a silence. It was not a nice thought

'I wonder how father found his hiding-place,' said George thoughtfully.

to think of Timmy at the wrong end of a gun. This had happened once or twice before in their adventures, and they didn't want to think of it happening again.

'Well, it's no good thinking silly things like that,' said Dick, getting up. 'We've had a jolly interesting half-hour. I think we've solved *that* mystery. But I suppose we shan't know for certain till your father's finished his experiment, George, and left the island—then we can go over and have a good snoop round.'

'It's still raining,' said Anne, looking out of the window. 'But it's a bit clearer. It looks as if the sun will be out soon. Let's go for a walk.'

'I shall go up to the coastguard's cottage,' said George, at once. 'I want to look through his telescope to see if I can just get a glimpse of Timmy.'

'Try the field-glasses,' suggested Julian. 'Go up to the top of the house with them.'

She fetched the field-glasses, where they hung in the hall, and took them out of their leather case. She ran upstairs with them. But she soon came down again, looking disappointed.

'The house isn't high enough for me to see much of the island properly. I can see the glass top of the tower easily, of course—but the telescope would show it much better. It's more powerful. I think I'll go up and have a squint. You don't need to come if you don't want to.' She put the glasses back into their case.

'Oh, we'll all come and have a squint for old Timmy dog,' said Dick, getting up. 'And I don't mind telling you what we'll see!'

'What?' said George, in surprise.

'We'll see Timmy having a perfectly wonderful time, chasing every single rabbit on the island!' said Dick with a grin. 'My word—you needn't worry about Timmy not having his food regularly! He'll have rabbit for breakfast, rabbit for dinner, rabbit for tea—and rainwater from his favourite pool. Not a bad life for old Timmy!'

'You know perfectly well he'll do nothing of the sort,' said George. 'He'll keep close to Father and not think of rabbits once!'

'You don't know Timmy if you think that,' said Dick dodging out of George's way. She was turning red with exasperation. 'I bet that's why he wanted to stay. *Just* for the rabbits!'

George threw a book at him. It crashed to the floor. Anne giggled. 'Oh stop it, you two. We'll never get out. Come on Ju—we won't wait for the squabblers!'

George threw a book at him. It crashed to the floor.

Chapter 13

Afternoon with Martin

JULIAN KNOCKED AND ENTERED...
IT'S US! CAN WE COME IN? WE HEARD YOU'D HAD AN ACCIDENT.
OH COME IN, DO! IT'S ALL RIGHT—IT'S JUST THAT I TWISTED MY ANKLE. SILLY THING TO DO!
OH—IT'LL SOON BE RIGHT IF IT'S JUST A TWIST. THE THING IS TO WALK ON IT AS SOON AS YOU CAN. WHERE WERE YOU WHEN YOU FELL?
WELL, ER— I WAS WALKING ON THE EDGE OF THE QUARRY WITH MY FATHER, AND I SLIPPED AND ROLLED A GOOD WAY DOWN.
I HOPE YOU DIDN'T GO AND GIVE AWAY OUR LITTLE SECRET? YOU DIDN'T TELL YOUR FATHER ABOUT THAT HOLE UNDER THE SHELF OF ROCK, DID YOU?
I—I'M AFRAID I DID. I DIDN'T THINK IT WOULD MATTER. I'M SORRY.
BLOW! WE WANTED TO GO AND EXPLORE IT THIS AFTERNOON, BUT WE THOUGHT IT WOULD BE SO WET WE'D FALL DOWN THE STEEP SLOPE.
I SUPPOSE THAT'S WHAT HAPPENED TO YOU? YOU TRIED CLAMBERING DOWN AND SLIPPED!
YES. I'M REALLY SORRY—I JUST MENTIONED IT TO MY FATHER OUT OF INTEREST, AND HE WANTED TO GO DOWN AND SEE FOR HIMSELF.
I SUPPOSE JOURNALISTS ARE ALWAYS LIKE THAT. WANTING TO BE ON THE SPOT IF THERE'S ANYTHING TO BE FERRETED OUT.
ALL RIGHT, MARTIN—FORGET IT. BUT DO TRY AND HEAD YOUR FATHER OFF THE QUARRY. WE WOULD LIKE TO DO A BIT OF EXPLORING, BEFORE HE BUTTS IN. THOUGH THERE MAY BE NOTHING TO BE FOUND AT ALL.
THEN THERE WAS A PAUSE. ANNE FELT QUITE SORRY FOR MARTIN...
AREN'T YOU BORED, LYING HERE?
YES, AWFULLY. I WANTED MY FATHER TO GO IN AND ASK THE COASTGUARD TO BRING IN SOME FIGURES I SAID I'D PAINT FOR HIM. BUT HE WOULDN'T.
YOU KNOW, I SIMPLY LOVE PAINTING—EVEN DOING A LITTLE THING LIKE THAT, PAINTING CLOTHES ON TOY PORTERS AND GUARDS...
OH—YOU WANT TO BE AN ARTIST! I WOULD LIKE THAT TOO!
ANNE! YOU CAN'T EVEN DRAW A CAT! AND WHEN YOU DREW A COW I THOUGHT IT WAS AN ELEPHANT!
I'LL SHOW YOU SOME OF MY PICTURES. I HAVE TO KEEP THEM HIDDEN AWAY, BECAUSE MY FATHER CAN'T BEAR ME TO WANT TO BE AN ARTIST!

DON'T GET UP—I'LL GET THEM FOR YOU.
IT'S ALL RIGHT. IF IT'S GOOD FOR ME TO TRY AND WALK, I WILL. THERE— NOT SO BAD AFTER ALL!
MARTIN LIMPED ACROSS TO THE BOOKCASE, AND FROM BEHIND IT HE PULLED OUT A CARD-BOARD CASE FULL OF PAINTINGS.
GRACIOUS! THEY'RE BEAUTIFUL! DID YOU REALLY DO THESE?
THEY ALL LOOKED IN SURPRISE. THIS WAS CERTAINLY GIFTED. WHY, THESE DRAWINGS WERE AS GOOD AS ANY THEY HAD EVER SEEN IN EXHIBITIONS!
DO YOU MEAN YOUR FATHER DOESN'T THINK THESE ARE GOOD— DOESN'T HE THINK IT'S WORTHWHILE TO LET YOU TRAIN AS AN ARTIST?
HE HATES MY PICTURES. HE THINKS IT'S A WEAK, FEEBLE THING FOR A MAN TO DO. SO I ONLY DO IT IN SECRET NOW.
POOR MARTIN! IT SEEMED AN AWFUL THING THAT A BOY WHO HAD NO MOTHER SHOULD HAVE A FATHER WHO HATED THE THING HIS SON MOST LOVED. NO WONDER HE ALWAYS LOOKED DULL AND MISERABLE AND SULLEN!
IT'S VERY BAD LUCK. I WISH WE COULD DO SOMETHING TO HELP.
WELL—GET ME THOSE FIGURES AND THE PAINT TINS FROM THE COAST-GUARD, WILL YOU? FATHER WON'T BE BACK TILL SIX.
AND DO STAY AND HAVE TEA WITH ME. IT'S SO DULL UP HERE. I HATE IT.
YES, I'LL GET THE THINGS FOR YOU. AND WE'LL RING UP MY AUNT AND TELL HER WE'RE STAYING FOR TEA—SO LONG AS WE DON'T EAT EVERYTHING YOU'VE GOT!
OH, THAT'S ALL RIGHT. THERE'S PLENTY OF FOOD IN THE HOUSE— MY FATHER HAS AN ENORMOUS APPETITE!
JULIAN WAS BACK IN NO TIME—AND WITH PAINTS AND BRUSHES TO WORK WITH, MARTIN SEEMED A DIFFERENT BOY!
THIS IS GRAND! IT'S A SILLY LITTLE JOB, THIS, BUT IT WILL HELP THE OLD MAN NEXT DOOR, AND I'M ALWAYS HAPPY WHEN I'M MESSING ABOUT WITH A BRUSH AND PAINTS!
MARTIN WAS VERY, VERY CLEVER AT PAINTING THE LITTLE FIGURES. HE WAS QUICK AND DEFT, AND ANNE SAT WATCHING HIM, QUITE FASCINATED, WHILE GEORGE WENT TO HUNT FOR THE TEA-THINGS...
BEFORE LONG THEY WERE SITTING ROUND, ENJOYING A DELICIOUS SPREAD...
I SAY, THIS IS REALLY GRAND! I WISH MY FATHER WASN'T COMING BACK TILL EIGHT.
BUT THEN...
BY THE WAY—WHERE'S THE DOG? I THOUGHT HE ALWAYS WENT EVERY-WHERE WITH YOU! WHERE'S TIMMY?

Chapter 14
A shock for George

Dick looked at George. He didn't think it would matter telling Martin where Timmy was, so long as George didn't give the *reason* why he had been left on the island.

But George was going to hold her tongue now. She looked at Martin and spoke quite airily. 'Oh, Timmy? We left him behind today. He's all right.'

'Gone out shopping with your mother, I suppose, hoping for a visit to the butcher's!' said Martin. This was the first joke he had ever made to the children, and though it was rather a feeble one they laughed heartily. Martin looked pleased. He began to try and think of another little joke, while his deft hands put reds and blues and greens on the little wooden figures.

They all had a huge tea. Then, when the clock said a quarter to six the girls carried the painted figures carefully back to the coastguard, who was delighted with them. Dick took back the little tins of paint, and the brush stuck in a jar of turpentine.

'Well now, he's clever that boy, isn't he?' said the coastguard, eyeing the figures in delight. 'Looks sort of miserable and sulky—but he's not a bad sort of boy!'

'I'll just have one more squint through your telescope,' said George, 'before it gets too dark.'

She tilted it towards her island. But once more there was no sign of Timmy, or of her father either. She looked for some time, and then went to join the others. She shook her head as they raised their eyebrows inquiringly.

The girls washed up the tea-things, and cleared away neatly. Nobody felt as if they wanted to wait and see Mr Curton. They didn't feel as if they liked him very much, now they knew how hard he was on Martin.

'Thanks for a lovely afternoon,' said Martin, limping to the door with them.

'Thanks for a lovely afternoon,' said Martin, limping to the door with them. 'I enjoyed my spot of painting, to say nothing of your company.'

'You stick out for your painting,' said Julian. 'If it's the thing you've *got* to do, and you know it, you must go all out for it. See?'

'Yes,' said Martin, and his face went sullen again. 'But there are things that make it difficult—things I can't very well tell you. Oh well—never mind! I dare say it will all come right one day, and I'll be a famous artist with pictures in the academy!'

'Come on, quickly,' said Dick, in a low voice to Julian. 'There's his father coming back!'

They hurried off down the cliff-path, seeing Mr Curton out of the corner of their eyes, coming up the other path.

'Horrid man!' said Anne. 'Forbidding Martin to do what he really longs to do. And he seemed so nice and jolly and all-over-us, didn't he?'

'Very all-over-us,' said Dick, smiling at Anne's new word. 'But there are a lot of people like that—one thing at home and quite another outside!'

'I hope Mr Curton hasn't been trying to explore that passage in the side of the quarry,' said George, looking back, and watching the man walk up to his back door. 'It would be too bad if he butted in and spoilt our fun. I mean—there may be nothing to discover at all—but it will be fun even finding there *is* nothing.'

'Very involved!' said Dick, with a grin. 'But I gather what you mean. I say, that was a good tea, wasn't it?'

'Yes,' said George, looking all round her in an absent-minded manner.

'What's up?' said Dick. 'What are you looking like that for?'

'Oh—how silly of me—I was just looking for Timmy,' said George. 'You know, I'm so used to him always being at my heels or somewhere near that I just can't get used to him not being here.'

'Yes, I feel a bit like that too,' said Julian. 'As if there was something missing all the time. Good old Tim! We shall miss him awfully, all of us—but you most of all, George.'

'Yes. Especially on my bed at night,' said George. 'I shan't be able to go to sleep for ages and ages.'

'I hope Mr Curton hasn't been trying to explore the passage.'

'I'll wrap a cushion up in a rug and plonk it down on your feet when you're in bed,' said Dick. 'Then it will feel like Timmy!'

'It won't! Don't be silly,' said George, rather crossly. 'And anyway it wouldn't *smell* like him. He's got a lovely smell.'

'Yes, a Timmy-smell,' agreed Anne. 'I like it too.'

The evening went very quickly, playing the endless game of monopoly again. Julian lay in bed later, watching for his uncle's signal. Needless to say, George was at the window too! They waited for half past ten.

'Now!' said Julian. And just as he spoke there came the first flash from the lantern in the tower.

'One,' counted George, 'two—three—four—five—six!' She waited anxiously to see if there were any more, but there weren't.

'Now you can go to bed in peace,' said Julian to George. 'Your father is all right, and that means that Timmy is all right too. Probably he has remembered to give Timmy a good supper and has had some himself as well!'

'Well, Timmy would soon remind him, if he forgot to feed him, that's one thing,' said George, slipping out of the room. 'Good night, Dick; good night, Ju! See you in the morning.'

And back she went to her own bed and snuggled down under the sheets. It was queer not to have Timmy on her feet. She tossed about for a while, missing him, and then fell asleep quite suddenly. She dreamed of her island. She was there with Timmy—and they were discovering ingots of gold down in the dungeon. What a lovely dream!

Next morning dawned bright and sunny again. The April sky was as blue as the forget-me-nots coming

She fell asleep quite suddenly.

out in the garden. George gazed out of the dining-room window at breakfast time wondering if Timmy was running about her island.

'Dreaming about Tim?' said Julian, with a laugh. 'Never mind—you'll soon see him, George. Another hour or so and you'll feast your eyes on him through the coastguard's telescope!'

'Do you really think you'll be able to make out Tim, if he's in the tower with your father at half past ten?' asked her mother. 'I shouldn't have thought you would be able to.'

'Yes, I shall, Mother,' said George. 'It's a very powerful telescope, you know. I'll just go up and make my bed, then I'll go up the cliff-path. Anyone else coming?'

'I want Anne to help me with some turning out,' said her mother. 'I'm looking out some old clothes to give to the vicar's wife for her jumble sale. You don't mind helping me, Anne, do you?'

'No, I'd like to,' said Anne at once. 'What are the boys going to do?'

'I think I must do a bit of my holiday work this morning,' said Julian, with a sigh. 'I don't want to—but I've kept on putting it off. You'd better do some too, Dick. You know what you are—you'll leave it all to the last day if you're not careful!'

'All right. I'll do some too,' said Dick. 'You won't mind scooting up to the coastguard's cottage alone, will you, George?'

'Not a bit,' said George. 'I'll come back just after half past ten, as soon as I've spotted Timmy and Father.'

She disappeared to make her bed. Julian and Dick went to fetch some books. Anne went to make her bed too, and then came down to help her aunt. In a few minutes George yelled good-bye and rushed out of the house.

'What a hurricane!' said her mother. 'It seems as if George never walks if she can possibly run. Now, Anne—put the clothes in three piles—the very old—the not so old—and the quite nice.'

Just before half past ten Julian went up to his window to watch for the signal from his uncle. He waited patiently. A few seconds after the half-hour the flashes came—one, two, three, four, five, six—good! Now George would settle down for the day. Perhaps they could go to the quarry in the afternoon. Julian went back to his books and was soon buried in them, with Dick grunting by his side.

At about five minutes to eleven there was the sound of running feet and panting breath. George appeared at the door of the sitting-room where the two boys were doing

In a few minutes George yelled good-bye and rushed out of the house.

their work. They looked up.

George was red in the face, and her hair was windblown. She fought to get her breath enough to speak. 'Julian! Dick! Something's happened—Timmy wasn't there!'

'What do you mean?' said Julian in surprise. George slumped down on a chair, still panting. The boys could see that she was trembling too.

'It's serious, Julian! I tell you Timmy wasn't in the tower when the signals came!'

'Well—it only means that your absent-minded father forgot to take him up with him,' said Julian, in his most sensible voice. 'What *did* you see?'

'I had my eye glued to the telescope,' said George, 'and suddenly I saw someone come into the little glass room at the top. I looked for Timmy, of course, at once—but I tell you, he wasn't there! The six flashes came, the man disappeared —and that was all. No Timmy! Oh I do feel so dreadfully worried, Julian.'

'Well, don't be,' said Julian, soothingly. 'Honestly, I'm sure that's what happened. Your father forgot about Timmy. Anyway, if you saw *him*, obviously things are all right.'

'I'm not thinking about Father!' cried George. 'He must be all right if he flashed his signals—I'm thinking about Timmy. Why, even if Father forgot to take him, he'd go with him. You know that!'

'Your father might have shut the door at the bottom and prevented Timmy from going up,' said Dick.

'He might,' said George, frowning. She hadn't thought of that. 'Oh dear—now I shall worry all day long. *Why* didn't I stay with Timmy? What shall I do now?'

'Wait till tomorrow morning,' said Dick. 'Then probably you'll see old Tim all right.'

'Tomorrow morning! Why, that's *ages* away!' said poor George. She put her head in her hands and groaned. 'Oh, nobody understands how much I love Timmy. You would perhaps if you had a dog of your own, Julian. It's an awful feeling, really. Oh Timmy, are you all right?'

She put her head in her hands and groaned. 'Oh, nobody understands how much I love Timmy.'

'Of course he's all right,' said Julian, impatiently. 'Do pull yourself together, George.'

'I *feel* as if something's wrong,' said George, looking obstinate. 'Julian—I think I'd better go across to the island.'

'No,' said Julian at once. 'Don't be idiotic, George. Nothing is wrong, except that your father's been forgetful. He's sent his OK signal. That's enough! You're not to go and create a scene over there with him. That would be disgraceful!'

'Well—I'll try and be patient,' said George, unexpectedly meek. She got up, looking worried. Julian spoke in a kinder voice.

'Cheer up, old thing! You do like to go off the deep end, don't you?'

Marvels in Miniature

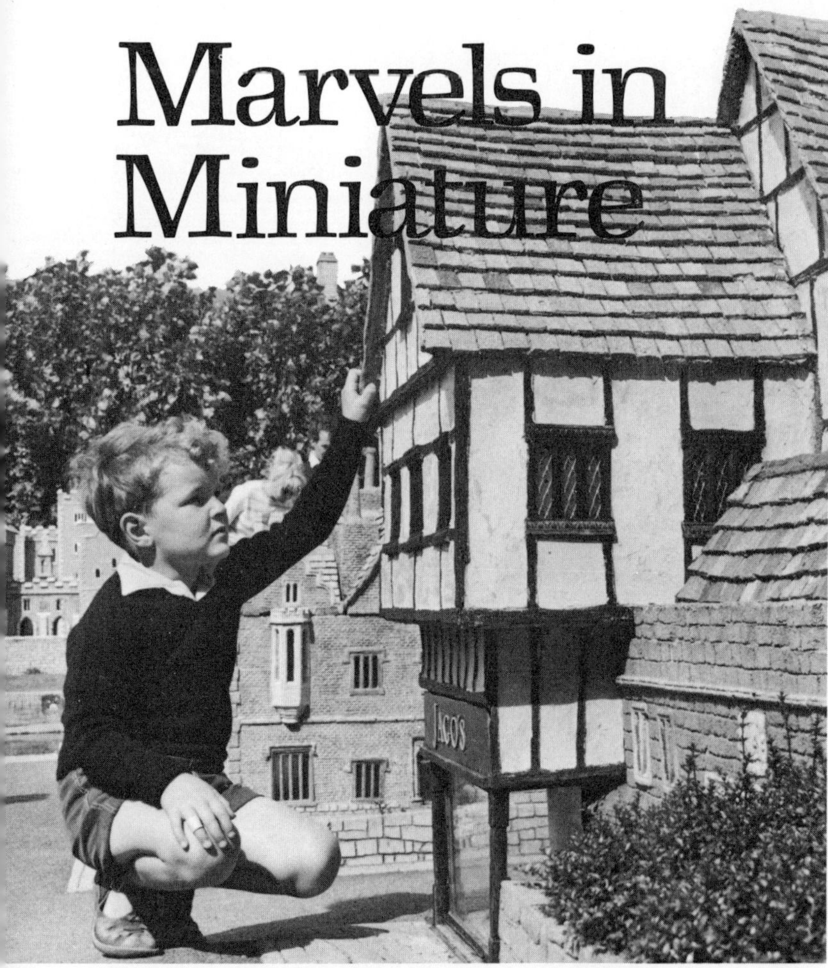

Above: Buildings in model villages are near perfect in scale and detail, as in this village in Weston-Super-Mare. Insert: Even model buildings need care and attention.

Small-scale models fascinate the four children, and they were thrilled to see the fine model toys their coastguard friend was making in his workshop on the cliff-top.

The very early modellers had to make their models from natural materials such as wood, stone, bone and clay. Later on they were able to make use of glass and various metals, including silver and gold.

Did you know that model soldiers have been popular since the time of the early Egyptians? They were placed in the tombs of kings to guard them in the next world! In the Cairo museum you can see a company of a dead Pharoah's army carved in wood.

Large-scale production of model soldiers began in the 18th century, particularly at Nuremburg, which has lots of lead mines close by. The earliest figures were very crude, but before long a tinsmith named Johan Hilbert set up a works producing lead soldiers which were perfect in form and colour. Within a few years the firm was making soldiers of 40 different types. A large number of outworkers were trained to paint the figures in their own houses.

The invention of the motor car gave model-making firms a new market to tackle. From a small beginning it grew into a mighty world-wide industry, and the perfection in detail of many of today's model cars is remarkable.

Another very popular 'marvel in miniature' is the model village, to be seen at many seaside resorts and tourist spots in Britain. Most of them are craftsman-built to scale and include churches, castles, shops, cottages and country mansions. You can walk along streets where house-tops are only shoulder high and see miniature gardens where even the trees and shrubs are miniature too.

Puzzle Page

The Five didn't let wet days worry them. If they had to stay indoors they had lots of fun with puzzles and brain-teasers of all descriptions. We could do the same, so here are a few to puzzle over on those 'indoor' days.

Time for Thought

(A) How many times does the minute hand of a clock pass the hour hand in twelve hours?

(B) An afternoon thunderstorm caused a power failure at 4.30 p.m. The next morning at 10 o'clock, the dial on the electric clock shows 2.30. How long was the electricity off? When did it come on again?

Animals in Your Garden

Hiding in your garden are lots of creatures, including some fierce ones! To find them, complete the clues.

1. SNAP.... 2. ....GLOVES. 3. DANDE.... 4. ....SLIPS. 5. ....WILLOWS. 6. ....WOOD. 7. ....LILY. 8. ....NIP. 9. ....BERRY BUSH. 10. ....WEED.

Answers on page 90.

A Postal Problem

Can you give the correct destination for a letter addressed as follows:

Wood Esq.
Dudley
Hampshire

Game Scrabble

Many sports and games are easily identified by only one word. Can you link these clues to the correct activity?

1. CHUKKER. 2. MALLET. 3. DRIVE. 4. BAILS. 5. PAWN. 6. PASS. 7. FOREHAND DRIVE. 8. BULLY-OFF. 9. SCRUM. 10. SHUTTLECOCK. 11. JUMP. 12. TRICK.

Word Diamond

First letter in *dear*
To drink slowly
Extra
Precious stone
Haughty
Stop
Last letter in *word*

Public Schools in Hiding

Each of the following suggests the name of a famous public school. Can you solve the clues?

1. A rifle. 2. Agricultural implement. 3. Done by doctors. 4. A ball game. 5. The 'Iron Duke'.

Musical Mix-Up

Hidden in the following groups of jumbled letters are the names of ten musical instruments. Can you sort them out?

1. OILVIN. 2. URITAG. 3. OPANI. 4. JONBA. 5. GROAN. 6. DACINOCOR. 7. PUTTMER. 8. MOBORTEN. 9. UFELT. 10. LOLCE.

Chapter 15

In the middle of the night

George did not moan any more about her worries. She went about with an anxious look in her blue eyes, but she had the sense not to tell her mother how worried she was at not seeing Timmy in the glass room, when her father signalled.

She mentioned it, of course, but her mother took the same view as Julian did. 'There! I knew he'd forget to take Timmy up! He's so very forgetful when he's at work.'

The children decided to go to the quarry that afternoon and explore the tunnel under the shelf of rock. So they set off after their lunch. But when they came to the quarry, they did not dare to climb down the steep sides. The heavy rain of the day before had made them far too dangerous.

'Look,' said Julian, pointing to where the bushes and smaller plants were ripped up and crushed. 'I bet that's where old Martin fell down yesterday! He might have broken his neck!'

'Yes. I vote we don't attempt to go down till it's as dry as it was the other day,' said Dick.

It was very disappointing. They had brought torches, and a rope, and had looked forward to a little excitement. 'Well, what shall we do?' asked Julian.

'I'm going back home,' said George, unexpectedly. 'I'm tired. You others go for a walk.'

Anne looked at George. She did seem rather pale. 'I'll come back with you, George,' said Anne slipping her hand through her cousin's arm. But George shook it off.

'No thanks, Anne. I really would rather be alone.'

'Well—we'll go over to the cliff then,' said Julian. "It'll be nice and blowy up there. See you later, George!'

They went off. George turned and sped back to Kirrin Cottage. Her mother was out. Joanna was upstairs in her bedroom. George went to the larder and took several things from it. She bundled them into a bag and then fled out of the house.

She found James the fisher-boy. 'James! You're not to tell a soul. I'm going over to Kirrin Island tonight—because I'm worried about Timmy. We left him there. Have my boat ready at ten o'clock.'

James was always ready to do anything in the world for George. He nodded and asked no questions at all. 'Right, Miss. It'll be ready. Anything you want put in it?'

'Yes, this bag,' said George. 'Now don't split on me, James. I'll be back tomorrow if I find Tim's all right.'

She fled back to the house. She hoped Joanna would not notice the things she had taken from the larder shelf.

'I can't help it if what I'm doing is wrong,' she kept whispering to herself. 'I know something isn't right with Timmy. And I'm not at all sure about Father, either. He *wouldn't* have forgotten his solemn promise to me about taking Timmy up with him. I'll have to go across to the island. I can't help it if it's wrong!'

The others wondered what was up with George when they came back

George went to the larder and took several things from it, and bundled them into a bag.

from their walk. She was so fidgety and restless. They had tea and then did some gardening for Aunt Fanny. George did some too, but her thoughts were far away, and twice her mother had to stop her pulling up seedlings instead of weeds.

Bedtime came. The girls got into bed at about a quarter to ten. Anne was tired and fell asleep at once. As soon as George heard her regular breathing she crept quietly out of bed and dressed again. She pulled on her warmest jersey, got her raincoat, rubber boots and a thick rug, and tiptoed downstairs.

Out of the side door she went and into the night. There was a bit of a moon in the sky, so it was not as dark as usual. George was glad. She would be able to see her way through the rocks a little now—though she was sure she could guide the boat even in the dark!

James was waiting for her. Her boat was ready. 'Everything's in,' said James. 'I'll push off. Now you be careful, Miss—and if you do scrape a rock, row like anything in case she fills and sinks. Ready?'

Off went George, hearing the lap-lap of the water against the sides of the boat. She heaved a sigh of relief, and began to row strongly away from the shore. She frowned as she rowed. Had she brought everything she might want? Two torches. Plenty of food. A tin-opener. Something to drink. A rug to wrap herself in tonight.

Back in Kirrin Cottage Julian lay in bed watching for his uncle's signal. Half past ten. Now for the signal. Ah, here they were! One—two—three—four—five—six! Good. Six and no more!

He wondered why George hadn't come into his and Dick's room to watch for them. She had last night. He got up, padded to the door of George's room and put his head in. 'George!' he said softly. 'It's OK. Your father's signals have just come again.'

There was no reply. Julian heard

Off went George, hearing the lap of the water against the boat.

regular breathing and turned to go back to bed. The girls must be asleep already! Well, George couldn't really be worrying much about Timmy now, then! Julian got into his bed and soon fell asleep himself. He had no idea that George's bed was empty—no idea that even now George was battling with the waves that guarded Kirrin Island!

It was more difficult that she had expected, for the moon did not really give very much light, and had an annoying way of going behind a cloud just when she badly needed every scrap of light she could get. But, deftly and cleverly, she managed to make her way through the passage between the hidden rocks. Thank goodness the tide was high so that most of them were well below the surface!

At last she swung her boat into the little cove. Here the water was perfectly calm. Panting a little, George pulled her boat up as far as she could. Then she stood in the darkness and thought hard.

What was she going to do? She did not know where her father's hiding-place was—but she felt certain the entrance to it must be somewhere in or near the little stone room. Should she make her way to that?

Yes, she would. It would be the only place to shelter in for the night, anyway. She would put on her torch when she got there, and hunt round for any likely entrance to the hiding-place. If she found it, she would go in—and what a surprise she would give her father! If old Timmy was there he would go mad with delight.

She took the heavy bag, draped the rug over her arm, and set off. She did not dare to put on her torch yet, in case the unknown enemy was lurking near. After all, her father had heard him cough at night!

George was not frightened. She did not even think about being frightened. All her thoughts were set on finding Timmy and making sure he was safe.

She began to search for the hiding-place.

She came to the little stone room. It was pitch-dark in there, of course—not even the faint light of the moon pierced into its blackness. George had to put on her torch.

She put down her bundle by the wall at the back, near the old fireplace recess. She draped the rug over it and sat down to have a rest, switching off her torch.

After a while she got up cautiously and switched on her torch again. She began to search for the hiding-place. Where *could* the entrance be? She flashed her torch on to every flagstone in the floor of the room. But not one looked as if it had been moved or lifted. There was nothing to show where there might be an entrance underground.

She moved round the walls—examining those too in the light of her torch. No—there was so sign that a hidden way lay behind any of those stones either. It was most tantalising. If she only knew!

She went to wrap the rug round her, and to sit and think. It was cold now. She was shivering, as she sat there in the dark, trying to puzzle out where the hidden entrance could be.

And then she heard a sound! She jumped and then stiffened all over, holding her breath painfully. What was it?

There was a curious grating noise. Then a slight thud. It came from the recess where people long ago had built their big log fires! George sat perfectly still, straining her eyes and ears.

She saw a beam of light in the fireplace recess. Then she heard a man's cough!

Was it her father? He had a cough at times. She listened hard. The beam of light grew brighter. Then she heard another noise—it sounded as if someone had jumped down from somewhere! And then—a voice!

'Come on!'

It was not her father's voice! George grew cold with fear then. Not her father's voice! Then what had happened to him—and to Timmy?

Someone else jumped down into the recess, grumbling. 'I'm not used to this crawling about!'

That wasn't her father's voice either. So there were *two* unknown enemies! Not one. And they knew her father's secret workroom. George felt almost faint with horror. Whatever had happened to him and Timmy?

The men walked out of the little stone room without seeing George at all. She guessed they were going to the tower. How long would they be? Long enough for her to search for the place they had appeared from?

She strained her ears again. She heard their footsteps going into the great yard. She tiptoed to the doorway and looked out. Yes—there was the light of their torch near the tower! If they were going up, there would be plenty of time to look round.

She went back into the little stone room. Her hands were trembling and she found it difficult to switch on her torch. She went to the fireplace recess and flashed the light in it.

She gave a gasp! Half way up the recess at the back was a black opening! She flashed the light up there. Evidently there was a movable stone half way up that swung back and revealed an entrance behind. An entrance to what? Were there steps such as were shown in the old map?

Feeling quite breathless, George stood on tip-toe and flashed her light into the hole. Yes—there were steps! They went down into the wall at the back. She remembered that the little stone room backed on to one of the immensely thick old walls still left.

She stood there, uncertain what to do. Had she better go down and see if she could find Timmy and her father? But if she did, she might be made a prisoner too. On the other hand, if she stayed outside, and the men came back and shut up the entrance, she might not be able to open it. She would be worse off than ever!

'I'll go down!' she suddenly decided. 'But I'd better take my bag and the rug, in case the men come back and see them. I don't want them to know I'm on the island if I can help it! I could hide them somewhere down there, I expect. I wonder if this entrance leads to the dungeons.'

She lifted up the rug and the bag and pushed them into the hole. She heard the bag roll down the steps, the tins inside making a muffled noise.

Then she climbed up herself. Gracious, what a long dark flight of steps! Wherever did they lead to?

Scheme for Survival

Can you remember what George took with her when she set out for Kirrin Island all alone in the middle of the night? She didn't have much time to plan her trip, but she did think to take two torches, some food and drink, warm clothing and a rug. I wonder what *you* would have taken.

On any adventure you tackle, it makes plain sense to start out prepared for the unexpected. Hopefully, your adventure will not turn out to be as dangerous as some that the Five have become involved in.

What must not be forgotten, is how nasty and unpredictable the weather can sometimes be, so always check the weather forecast before you set off. If you do decide to get away from civilisation for a while, do make certain that you are well prepared. Here are a few tips to help you.

Pack a basic survival kit. This should always include the following:

First-aid kit
Local map and compass
Spare warm clothes
Torch
Matches
Food (chocolate, glucose, etc)
Spare blanket
Whistle
'Space' blanket (from camping shop) or plastic sheet
Length of strong twine

Your first-aid kit should include large plasters, cotton wool, tube of medical cream, bandages, safety pins, and scissors. If an accident should occur, use your commonsense and don't panic. Better still, study some first-aid beforehand so that you will know how to cope with shock, unconsciousness, hypothermia (exposure), heavy bleeding, and if someone stops breathing.

Make sure you know how to use the map and compass too. And if you should lose your compass, remember you can still find the direction of south by the hands of a watch during the day (the sun is always due south at noon — or 1pm summer-time).

Wear or carry sensible clothing too. You may only need lightweight summer clothing to begin with, but the weather can change rapidly, especially in mountainous areas. Make sure you have something to keep out the wind and rain, plus a hat and gloves. Proper walking boots are also essential, especially for long hikes.

Finally, the most important points of all:

Never go alone. Take two, or preferably three, friends along with you, so that if one of you should have an accident, someone can stay with the injured person while the others go for help.

Always tell someone that you are going on a ramble, hill-trek or whatever, and which route you intend to take.

Don't be careless. More accidents are caused by carelessness than for any other reason.

If you bear all these things in mind, you can plan really exciting expeditions with your friends in complete safety.

Have a good time!

Chapter 16

Down to the caves

George went cautiously down the stone steps. They were steep and narrow. 'I should think they run right down in the middle of the stone wall,' thought George. 'Goodness, here's a narrow bit!'

It was so narrow that she had to go sideways. 'A fat man would never get through there!' she thought to herself. 'Hallo—the steps have ended!'

She had got the rug round her shoulders, and had picked up her bag on the way down. In her other hand she held her torch. It was terribly dark and quiet down there. George did not feel scared because she was hoping to see Timmy at any moment. No one could feel afraid with Timmy just round the corner, ready to welcome them!

She stood at the bottom of the steps, her torch showing her a narrow tunnel. It curved sharply to the left. 'Now will it join the dungeons from here?' she wondered, trying to get her sense of direction to help her. 'They can't be far off. But there's no sign of them at the moment.'

It was terribly dark and quiet down there.

She went on down the narrow tunnel. Once the roof came down so low she almost had to crawl. She flashed her torch on it. She saw black rock there, which had evidently been too hard to be removed by the tunnel-builders long ago.

The tunnel went on and on and on. George was puzzled. Surely by now she must have gone by all the dungeons! Why—she must be heading towards the shore of the island! How very queer! Didn't this tunnel join the dungeons then? A little further and she would be under the bed of the sea itself.

The tunnel took a deep slope downwards. More steps appeared, cut roughly from rock. George climbed down them cautiously. Where in the world was she going?

At the bottom of the steps the tunnel seemed to be cut out of solid rock—or else it was a natural passage, not made by man at all. George didn't know. Her torch showed her black, rocky walls and roof, and her feet stumbled over an irregular rocky path. How she longed for Timmy beside her!

'I must be very deep down,' she thought, pausing to flash her torch round her once more. 'Very deep down and very far from the castle! Good gracious—whatever's that awful noise?'

She listened. She heard a muffled booming and moaning. Was it her father doing one of his experiments? The noise went on and on, a deep, never-ending boom.

'Why—I believe it's the sea!' said George, amazed. She stood and listened again. 'Yes—it *is* the sea—over my head! I'm under the rocky bed of Kirrin Bay!'

And now poor George did feel a bit scared! She thought of the great waves surging above her, she thought of the restless, moving water scouring the rocky bed over her head, and felt frightened in case the sea should find a way to leak down into her narrow tunnel!

'Now don't be silly,' she told herself sternly. 'This tunnel has been here under the sea-bed for hundreds of years—why should it suddenly become unsafe just when *you* are in it, George?'

Talking to herself like this, to keep up her spirits, she went on again. It was very queer indeed to think she was walking under the sea. So this was where her father was at work! Under the sea itself.

And then George suddenly remembered something he had said to them all, the first time they had visited him on the island. What was it now? 'Oh yes! He said he had to have water *above* and *around* him!' said George. '*Now* I see what he meant! His workroom is somewhere down here—so the sea-water is *above* him—and it's all *round* the tower, because it's built on an island!'

Water above and water around—so that was why her father had chosen Kirrin Island for his experiment. How had he found the secret passage under the sea, though? 'Why, even I didn't know of that,' said George. 'Hallo—what am I coming to?'

She stopped. The passage had suddenly widened out into an enormous dark cave, whose roof was unexpectedly high, lost in dark shadows. George stared round. She saw queer things there that she didn't understand at all—wires, glass boxes, little machines that seemed to be at work without a sound, whose centres were alive with queer, gleaming, shivering light.

Sudden sparks shot up now and again, and when that happened a funny smell crept round the cave. 'How weird all this is!' thought George. 'However can Father understand all these machines and things! I wonder where he is. I do hope those men haven't made him prisoner somewhere!'

From this queer, Aladdin's cave another tunnel led. George switched on her torch again and went into it. It was much like the other one, but the roof was higher.

Sitting at the table his head in his hands, perfectly still, was her father!

She came to another cave, smaller this time, and crammed with wires of all kinds. There was a curious humming sound here, like thousands of bees in a hive. George half-expected to see some flying round.

'It must be these wires making the noise,' she said. There was nobody in the cave at all, but it led into another one, and George hoped that soon she would find Timmy and her father.

She went into the next cave, which was perfectly empty and very cold. She shivered. Then down another passage, and into a small cave. The first thing she saw beyond this tiny cave was a light!

A light! Then perhaps she was coming to the cave her father must be in! She flashed her torch round the little cave she was now standing in, and saw tins of food, bottles of beer, tins of sweets, and a pile of clothes of some sort. Ah, this was where her father kept his stores. She went on to the next cave, wondering why Timmy had not heard her and come to greet her.

She looked cautiously into the cave where the light came from. Sitting at a table, his head in his hands, perfectly still, was her father! There was no sign of Timmy.

'Father!' said George. The man at the table jumped violently and turned round. He stared at George as if he really could not believe his eyes. Then he turned back again, and buried his face in his hands.

'*Father!*' said George again, quite frightened because he did not say anything to her.

He looked round again, and this time he got up. He stared at George once more, and then sat down heavily. George ran to him. 'What's the matter? Oh Father, what's the matter? Where's Timmy?'

'George! Is it *really* you, George? I

thought I must be dreaming when I looked up and saw you!' said her father. 'How did you get here? Good gracious, it's impossible that you should be here!'

'Father, are you all right? What's happened—and where's Timmy?' said George, urgently. She looked all round, but could see no sign of him. Her heart went cold. Surely nothing awful had happened to Timmy?

'Did you see two men?' asked her father. 'Where were they?'

'Oh Father—we keep asking each other questions and not answering them!' said George. 'Tell me first —where is Timmy?'

'I don't know,' said her father. 'Did those two men go to the tower?'

'Yes,' said George. 'Father, what's happened?'

'Well, if they've gone to the tower, we've got about an hour in peace,' said her father. 'Now, listen to me, George, very carefully. This is terribly important.'

'I'm listening,' said George. 'But do hurry up and tell me about Timmy.'

'These two men were parachuted down on to the island, to try and find out my secret,' said her father. 'I'll tell you what my experiments are for, George—they are to find a way of replacing all coal, coke and oil—an idea to give the world all the heat and power it wants, and to do away with mines and miners.'

'Good gracious!' said George. 'It would be one of the most wonderful things the world has ever known.'

'Yes,' said her father. 'And I should *give* it to the whole world—it shall not be in the power of any one country, or collection of men. It shall be a gift to the whole of mankind—but, George, there are men who want my secret for themselves, so that they may make colossal fortunes out of it.'

'How hateful!' cried George. 'Go on, Father—how did they hear of it?'

'Well, I was at work on this idea

'Did you see the two men? Where were they?'

with some of my colleagues, my fellow-workers,' said her father. 'And one of them betrayed us, and went to some powerful business men to tell them of my idea. So when I knew this I decided to come away in secret and finish my experiments by myself. Then nobody could betray me.'

'And you came here!' said George. 'To my island.'

'Yes—because I needed water over me and water around me,' said her father. 'Quite by chance I looked at a copy of that old map, and thought that if the passage shown there—the one leading from the little stone room, I mean—if the passage there *really* did lead under the sea, as it seemed to show, that would be the ideal place to finish my experiments.'

'Oh Father—and I made such a fuss!' said George, ashamed now to remember how cross she had been.

'Did you?' said her father, as if he had forgotten all about that. 'Well, I got all my stuff and came here. And now these fellows have found me, and got hold of me!'

'Poor Father! Can't I help?' said George. 'I could go back and bring help over here, couldn't I?'

'Yes, you could!' said her father. 'But you mustn't let those men see you, George.'

'I'll do anything you want me to, Father, anything!' said George. 'But first do tell me what's happened to Timmy?'

'Well, he kept by me all the time,' said her father. 'Really, he's a wonderful dog, George. And then, this morning, just as I was coming out of the entrance in that little room to go up into the tower with Timmy to signal, the two men pounced on me and forced me back here.'

'But what happened to Timmy?' asked George, impatiently. Would her father *never* tell her what she wanted to know?

'He flew at the men, of course,' said her father. 'But somehow or other one of them lassoed him with a noose of rope and caught him. They pulled the rope so tight round his neck that he almost choked.'

'Oh, poor, poor Timmy,' said George, and the tears ran down her cheeks. 'Is he—do you think—he's all right, Father?'

'Yes. From what I heard the men saying afterwards I think they've taken him to some cave and shut him in there,' said her father. 'Anyway, I saw one of them getting some dog-biscuits out of a bag this evening—so that looks as if he's alive and kicking—and hungry!'

George heaved a great sigh of relief. So long as Timmy was alive and all right! She took a few steps towards what she thought must be another cave. 'I'm going to find Timmy, Father,' she said. 'I *must* find him!'

Sea and Seaside Quiz

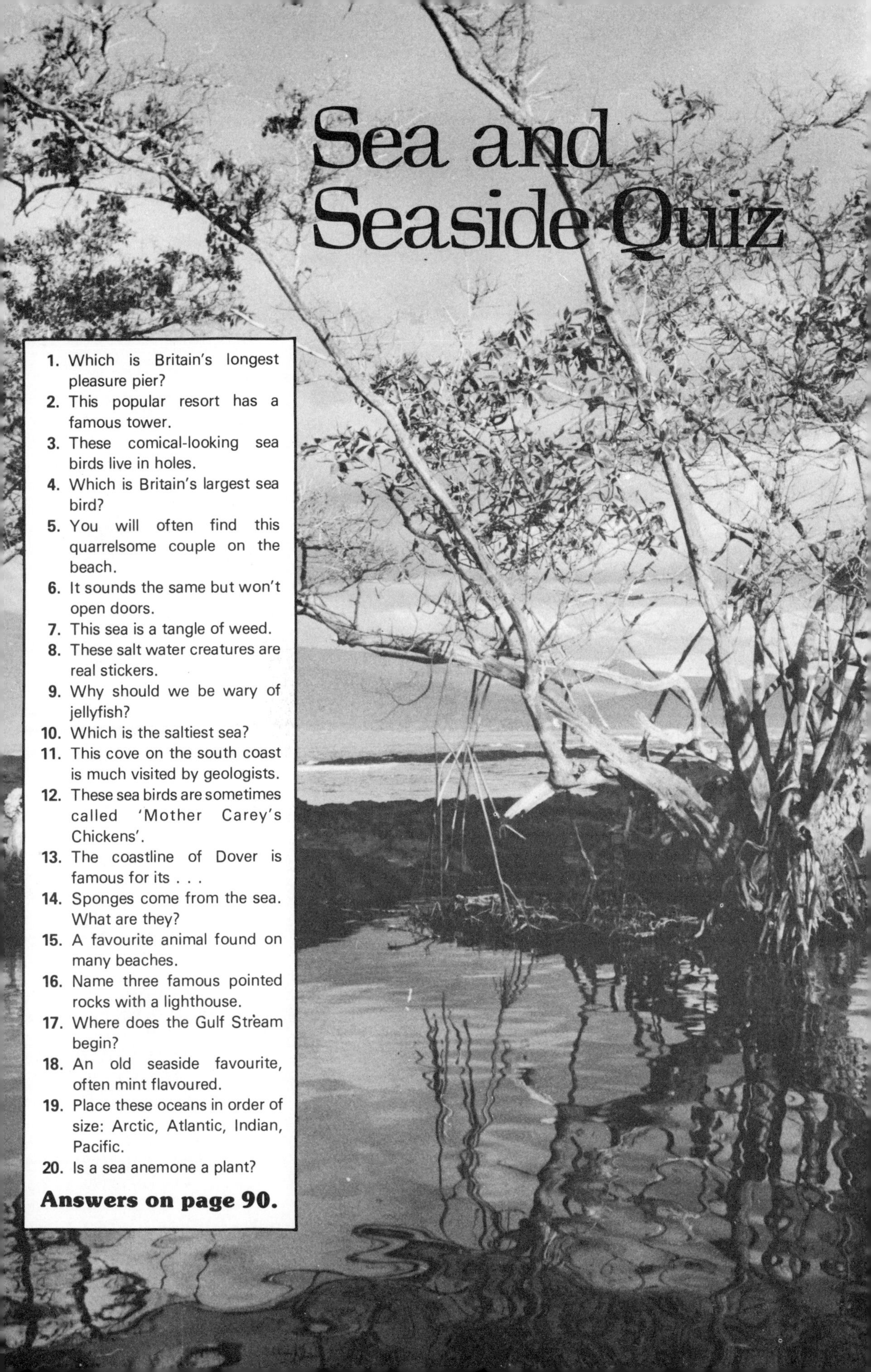

1. Which is Britain's longest pleasure pier?
2. This popular resort has a famous tower.
3. These comical-looking sea birds live in holes.
4. Which is Britain's largest sea bird?
5. You will often find this quarrelsome couple on the beach.
6. It sounds the same but won't open doors.
7. This sea is a tangle of weed.
8. These salt water creatures are real stickers.
9. Why should we be wary of jellyfish?
10. Which is the saltiest sea?
11. This cove on the south coast is much visited by geologists.
12. These sea birds are sometimes called 'Mother Carey's Chickens'.
13. The coastline of Dover is famous for its . . .
14. Sponges come from the sea. What are they?
15. A favourite animal found on many beaches.
16. Name three famous pointed rocks with a lighthouse.
17. Where does the Gulf Stream begin?
18. An old seaside favourite, often mint flavoured.
19. Place these oceans in order of size: Arctic, Atlantic, Indian, Pacific.
20. Is a sea anemone a plant?

Answers on page 90.

Chapter 17

Timmy at last

'Honestly, George, you do behave as bravely as any boy. I'm proud of you,' said her father.

'No, George!' called her father sharply. 'Come back. There is something very important I want to say. Come here!'

George went over to him, filled with impatience to get to Timmy, wherever he was. She *must* find him!

'Now listen,' said her father. I have a book in which I have made all my notes of this great experiment. The men haven't found it! I want you to take it safely to the mainland, George. Don't let it out of your sight! If the men get hold of it they would have all the information they needed!'

'But don't they know everything just by looking at your wires and machines and things?' asked George.

'They know a very great deal,' said her father, 'and they've found out a lot more since they've been here—but not quite enough. I daren't destroy my book of notes, because if anything should happen to me, my great idea would be completely lost. So, George, I must entrust it to you and you must take it to an address I will give you, and hand it to the person there.'

'It's an awful responsibility,' said George, a little scared of handling a book which meant so much, not only to her father, but possibly to the whole of the world. 'But I'll do my best, Father. I'll hide in one of the caves till the men come back, and then I'll slip back up the passage to the hidden entrance, get out, go to my boat and row back to the mainland. Then I'll deliver your book of notes without fail, and get help sent over here to you.'

'Good girl,' said her father, and gave her a hug. 'Honestly, George, you do behave as bravely as any boy. I'm proud of you.'

George thought that was the nicest thing her father had ever said to her. She smiled at him. 'Well, Father, I'll go and see if I can find Timmy now. I simply must see

George tugged at the stone with all her strength.

that he's all right before I go and hide in one of the other caves.'

'Very well,' said her father. 'The man who took the biscuits went in that direction—still further under the sea, George. Oh—by the way—how is it you're here in the middle of the night?'

It seemed to strike her father for the first time that George also might have a story to tell. But George felt that she really couldn't waste any more time—she *must* find Timmy!

'I'll tell you later, Father,' she said. 'Oh—where's that book of notes?'

Her father rose and went to the back of the cave. He took a box and stood on it. He ran his hand along a dark ridge of rock, and felt about until he had found what he wanted.

He brought down a slim book, whose pages were of very thin paper. He opened the book and George saw many beautifully drawn diagrams, and pages of notes in her father's small, neat handwriting.

'Here you are,' said her father, handing her the book 'do the best you can. If anything happens to me, this book will still enable my fellow-workers to give my idea to the world. If I come through this all right, I shall be glad to have the book, because it will mean I shall not have to work out all my experiments again.'

George took the precious book. She stuffed it into her macintosh pocket, which was a big one. 'I'll keep it safe, Father. Now I must go and find Timmy, or those two men will be back before I can hide in one of the other caves.'

She left her father's cave and went into the next one. There was nothing there at all. Then on she went down a passage that twisted and turned in the rock.

And then she heard a sound she longed to hear. A whine! Yes, really a whine!

'Timmy!' shouted George, eagerly. 'Oh Timmy! I'm coming!'

Timmy's whine stopped suddenly. Then he barked joyously. 'Woof, woof, woof, woof!' George almost fell as she tried to run down the narrow tunnel. Her torch showed her a big boulder that seemed to be blocking up a small cave in the side of the tunnel. Behind the boulder Timmy barked, and scraped frantically!

George tugged at the stone with all her strength. 'Timmy!' she panted. 'Timmy! I'll get you out! I'm coming! Oh, Timmy!'

The stone moved a little. George tugged again. It was almost too heavy for her to move at all, but despair made her stronger than she had ever been in her life. The stone quite suddenly swung to one side, and George just got one of her feet out of its way in time, or it would have been crushed.

Timmy squeezed out of the space left. He flung himself on George, who fell on the ground with her arms tight round him. He licked her face and whined, and she buried her nose in his thick fur in joy. 'Timmy! What have they done to you? Timmy, I came as soon as I could!'

Timmy whined again and again in joy, and tried to paw and lick George as if he couldn't have enough of her. It would have been difficult to say which of the two was the happier.

At last George pushed Timmy away firmly. 'Timmy we've got work to do! We've got to escape from here and get across to the mainland and bring help.'

'Woof,' said Timmy. George stood up and flashed her torch into the tiny cave where Timmy had been. She saw that there was a bowl of water there and some biscuits. The men had not ill-treated him, then, except to lasso him and half-choke him when they caught him. She felt round his neck tenderly, but except for a swollen ridge there, he seemed none the worse.

'Now hurry up—we'll go back to Father's cave—and then find another cave beyond his to hide in till the two men come back from the tower. Then we'll creep out into the little stone room and row back to the mainland,' said George. 'I've got a very, very important book here in my pocket, Timmy.'

Timmy growled suddenly, and the hairs on the back of his neck rose up. George stiffened, and stood listening.

A stern voice came down the passage. 'I don't know who you are or where you've come from—but if you have dared to let that dog loose he'll be shot! And, to show you that I mean what I say, here's something to let you know I've a revolver!'

Then there came a deafening crash, as the man pulled the trigger, and a bullet hit the roof somewhere in the passage. Timmy and George almost jumped out of their skins. Timmy would have leapt up the passage at once, but George had her hand on his collar. She was very frightened, and tried hard to think what was best to do.

The echoes of the shot went on and on. It was horrid. Timmy stopped growling, and George stayed absolutely still.

'Well?' said the voice, 'Did you hear what I said? If that dog is loose, he'll be shot. I'm not having my plans spoilt now. And you, whoever you are, will please come up the tunnel and let me see you. But I warn you—if the dog's with you, that's the end of him!'

'Timmy! Timmy, run away and hide somewhere!' whispered George suddenly. And then she remembered something else that filled her with despair. She had her father's precious book of notes with her—in her pocket! Suppose the man found it on her? It would break her father's heart to know that his wonderful secret had been stolen from him after all.

George hurriedly took the thin, flat little book from her pocket. She pushed it at Timmy. 'Put it in your mouth. Take it with you, Tim. And go and hide till it's safe to come. Quick! Go, Timmy, go! I'll be all right.'

To her great relief Timmy, with the book in his mouth, turned and disappeared down the tunnel that led further under the sea. How she

hoped he would find a safe hiding place! The tunnel must end soon —but maybe before it did, Timmy would settle down in some dark corner and wait for her to call him again.

'Will you come up the passage or not?' shouted the voice angrily. 'You'll be sorry if I have to come and fetch you—because I shall shoot all the way along!'

'I'm coming!' called George, in a small voice, and she went up the passage. She soon saw a beam of light, and in a moment she was in the flash of a powerful torch. There was a surprised exclamation.

'Good heavens! A boy! What are *you* doing here, and where did you come from?'

George's short curly hair made the man with the torch think she was a boy, and George did not tell him he was wrong. The man held a revolver, but he let it drop as he saw George. 'I only came to rescue my dog, and to find my father,' said George, in a meek voice.

'Well, you can't move that heavy stone!' said the man. 'A kid like you

'Good heavens! A boy! What are you doing here?'

wouldn't have the strength. And you can't rescue your father either! We've got him prisoner, as you no doubt saw.'

'Yes,' said George, delighted to think that the man was sure she had not been strong enough to move the big stone. She wasn't going to say a word about Timmy! If the man thought he was still shut up in that tiny cave, well and good!

Then she heard her father's voice, anxiously calling from somewhere beyond the man. 'George! Is that you? Are you all right?'

'Yes, Father!' shouted back George, hoping that he would not ask anything about Timmy. The man beckoned her to come to him. Then he pushed her in front of him and they walked to her father's cave.

'I've brought your boy back,' said the man. 'Silly little idiot—thinking he could set that savage dog free! We've got him penned up in a cave with a big boulder in front!'

Another man came in from the opposite end of the cave. He was amazed to see George. The other man explained.

'When I got down here, I heard a noise out beyond this cave, the dog barking and someone talking to him—and found this kid there, trying to set the dog free. I'd have shot the dog, of course, if he *had* been freed.'

'But—how did this boy get here?' asked the other man, still amazed.

'Maybe *he* can tell us that!' said the other. And then, for the first time, George's father heard how George had got there and why.

She told them how she had watched for Timmy in the glass room of the tower and hadn't seen him—and that had worried her and made her suspicious. So she had come across to the island in her boat at night, and had seen where the men came from. She had gone down the tunnel, and kept on till she came to the cave, where she had found her father.

The man pushed her in front of him.

The three men listened in silence. 'Well, you're a tiresome nuisance,' one of the men said to George, 'but my word, you're a son to be proud of. It's not many boys would have been brave enough to run so much risk for anyone.'

'Yes. I'm really proud of you, George,' said her father. He looked at her anxiously. She knew what he was thinking—what about his precious book? Had she been sensible enough to hide it? She did not dare to let him know anything while the men were there.

'Now, this complicates matters,' said the other man, looking at George. 'If you don't go back home you'll soon be missed, and there will be all kinds of search-parties going on—and maybe someone will send over to the island here to tell your father you have disappeared! We don't want anyone here at present —not till we know what we want to know!'

He turned to George's father. 'If you will tell us what we want to know, and give us all your notes, we will set you free, give you whatever sum of money you ask us for, and disappear ourselves.'

'And if I say I won't?' said George's father.

'Then I am afraid we shall blow up the whole of your machines and the tower—and possibly you will never be found again because you will be buried down here,' said the man, in a voice that was suddenly very hard.

There was a dead silence. George looked at her father. 'You couldn't do a thing like that,' he said at last. 'You would gain nothing by it at all!'

'It's all or nothing with us,' said the man. 'All or nothing. Make up your mind. We'll give you till half past ten tomorrow morning—about seven hours. Then either you tell us everything, or we blow the island sky-high!'

They went out of the cave and left George and her father together. Only seven hours! And then, perhaps, the end of Kirrin Island!

Spotlight on Castles

Take a castle, an island, and the Five on holiday, and you have all the ingredients for an exciting story. The old castle on Kirrin Island certainly gave the Five some thrilling adventures they will never forget!

Castles fascinate most of us. Their massive walls and weather-beaten stones give them an air of mystery and excitement. For centuries past they have been standing guard during times of war and peace, and providing the setting for some of the most important events in Britain's history.

The majority of our castles were built with the idea of making the task of the attackers as difficult as possible. For this reason they were usually set on top of a hill, or on steeply rising ground. The first obstacle to halt the attackers was a deep moat. Behind this lay the massive, thick outer wall. If the enemy succeeded in crossing the drawbridge over the moat they were confronted by a heavy wooden door. Behind this was a massive iron grating, the portcullis, dropped down into a narrow passageway to bar their progress. They also had to watch out for cascades of molten lead or pitch, showered down from the battlements! A castle could often withstand a siege for weeks or months on end.

If castles were so strongly constructed, why are many now in ruins? The chief reason is that after the Civil War Oliver Cromwell ordered that their roofs should be stripped, their battlements destroyed and the fortresses made unfit for defence purposes.

Fortunately, many castles have survived and been carefully restored. Some are still the homes of famous families whilst others, like the Tower of London, are museums and show-places.

Berkeley Castle, in the county of Gloucestershire, has been the fortress home of the Berkeley family for more than 800 years. It was in this castle that Edward II was imprisoned and finally put to death by means of red-hot rapiers.

Another fabulous fortress still inhabited is Warwick Castle, magnificent palace of the Earls of Warwick. It stands proudly on a cliff overlooking the River Avon. This Norman castle has passed through many periods of stirring history and although damaged by Cromwell it has risen again to become one of the great show-places of Britain.

Two of Britain's most famous 'lived-in' castles are Windsor and Glamis. Windsor is Britain's grandest and best-preserved castle and has been used as a royal residence for centuries past. It dates back to about the year 1070 and was one of a chain of castles built around London by William the Conqueror. It has had a fairly peaceful existence, having only been besieged on two occasions — in 1193 and 1215. Down the ages various sovereigns have spent vast sums of money improving the castle.

Glamis Castle, in Scotland, was the childhood home of Queen Elizabeth, the Queen Mother. Some of the oldest parts of the castle have walls over four metres thick! Now the seat of the Earl of Strathmore, the castle is said to have at least 300 rooms and — like Windsor — lots of ghosts!

Bamburgh castle, on the coast of Northumberland, stands on a rock that has been the site of fortresses since Stone Age times.

Chapter 18

Half past four in the morning

JULIAN WAS ASLEEP. SO WERE THE OTHERS, SO NOBODY GUESSED THAT GEORGE'S BED WAS EMPTY. BUT, ABOUT HALF PAST FOUR ANNE AWOKE, FEELING VERY HOT...
I REALLY MUST OPEN THE WINDOW— I'M BOILING!
IT WAS A BEAUTIFUL NIGHT. THE STARS WERE OUT AND THE BAY SHONE FAINTLY...
GEORGE— ARE YOU AWAKE?
NO REPLY CAME— NOT EVEN THE SOUND OF BREATHING! SHE FELT THE BED— NO GEORGE! QUICKLY, ANNE SWITCHED ON THE TABLE-LAMP...
OH! GEORGE HAS GONE TO THE ISLAND! ALL IN THE DARK BY HERSELF!
SHE WENT TO THE BOYS' ROOM AND SHOOK JULIAN AWAKE...
WHAT IS IT? WHAT'S UP?
JULIAN! GEORGE IS GONE. HER BED'S NOT BEEN SLEPT IN.
JULIAN REACHED FOR THE LIGHT— AND THEN DICK WAS AWAKE TOO...
BLOW! I MIGHT HAVE GUESSED SHE'D DO A FOOLISH THING LIKE THAT. IN THE MIDDLE OF THE NIGHT TOO— AND ALL THOSE DANGEROUS ROCKS TO ROW ROUND. NOW WHAT ARE WE GOING TO DO ABOUT IT?
THEY EXPLAINED TO DICK...
WELL, WE CAN'T DO ANYTHING NOW, CAN WE? NO DOUBT SHE'S ON KIRRIN ISLAND BY NOW, MAKING A FUSS OF TIMMY AND HAVING A GOOD OLD ROW WITH UNCLE QUENTIN! REALLY, GEORGE IS THE LIMIT!
THEY TALKED FOR A FURTHER HALF AN HOUR, AND THEN—
FIVE O'CLOCK. WE'D BETTER TRY AND GET A BIT MORE SLEEP. AUNT FANNY WILL BE WORRIED IN THE MORNING WHEN SHE HEARS OF GEORGE'S LATEST ESCAPADE!
THEY ALL WENT BACK TO BED, BUT JULIAN COULD NOT SLEEP, WONDERING ABOUT GEORGE. WAS SHE ALL RIGHT? AND THEN, SUDDENLY, HE HEARD A STRANGE NOISE DOWNSTAIRS...
WHATEVER WAS THAT? SOUNDED LIKE SOMEONE CLIMBING IN AT A WINDOW. SURELY IT ISN'T A BURGLAR, MAKING ALL THAT NOISE!
JULIAN SWITCHED ON THE LIGHT— AND AT THAT VERY MOMENT THE BEDROOM DOOR WAS PUSHED OPEN...
TIMMY! HOW DID YOU GET HERE? WHERE'S GEORGE? TIMMY, IS IT REALLY YOU?

A MOMENT LATER DICK WAS AWAKE...
TIMMY! HAS GEORGE BROUGHT HIM BACK THEN? IS SHE HERE TOO?
NO, APPARENTLY NOT. I THINK THE WINDOW IN THE LITTLE WASH-PLACE WAS LEFT OPEN—HE MUST HAVE COME THROUGH THERE. IS THAT IT, TIM?
SECONDS LATER, ANNE JOINED THEM...
WHY, TIMMY! OH JULIAN, IS GEORGE BACK TOO?
IT SEEMS NOT. I SAY, TIM, WHAT'S THIS YOU'VE GOT? DROP IT, OLD CHAP, DROP IT!
IT'S A BOOK OF NOTES—ALL IN UNCLE'S HAND-WRITING! WHAT DOES THIS MEAN? HOW DID TIMMY GET HOLD OF IT—AND WHY DID HE BRING IT HERE?
IT'S VERY QUEER. THERE'S SOMETHING I DON'T UNDER-STAND HERE. LET'S GO AND WAKE AUNT FANNY.
AUNT FANNY WAS VERY WORRIED INDEED TO HEAR THAT GEORGE WAS GONE—AND QUITE MYSTIFIED TO SEE HER HUSBAND'S BOOK OF NOTES...
I MUST PUT THIS INTO THE SAFE. I KNOW THIS IS VALUABLE. HOW DID TIMMY GET HOLD OF IT?
TIMMY WAS ACTING QUEERLY. HE KEPT PAWING AT JULIAN AND WHINING...
WHAT IS IT, OLD BOY? HOW DID YOU GET HERE? YOU DIDN'T SWIM, BECAUSE YOU'RE NOT WET. IF YOU CAME IN A BOAT IT MUST HAVE BEEN WITH GEORGE—AND YET YOU'VE LEFT HER BEHIND!
I THINK SOMETHING'S HAPPENED TO GEORGE. I THINK TIMMY KEEPS PAWING YOU TO TELL YOU TO GO WITH HIM AND FIND HER. WE OUGHT TO GO AND SEE.
YES, I THINK WE OUGHT. AUNT FANNY, WOULD YOU LIKE TO WAKE JOANNA AND GET SOMETHING HOT READY, IN CASE WE FIND GEORGE IS TIRED OUT AND COLD?
IT WILL SOON BE DAYLIGHT NOW. WE CAN GO DOWN TO THE BEACH AND LOOK.
WELL GO AND DRESS THEN. OH, WHAT A DREAD-FUL FAMILY I'VE GOT—ALWAYS IN SOME SCRAPE OR OTHER!
MINUTES LATER THEY WERE ALL DRESSED AND READY TO HEAD FOR THE BEACH. BUT TIMMY STARTED GOING IN THE OPPOSITE DIRECTION!
WHY—HE DOESN'T WANT US TO GO TO THE BEACH! HE WANTS US TO GO ANOTHER WAY! ALL RIGHT, TIMMY—YOU LEAD THE WAY AND WE'LL FOLLOW!

Chapter 19

A meeting with Martin

Timmy went straight to the shelf of rock and disappeared underneath it.

Timmy ran round the house and made for the moor behind. It was most extraordinary. Wherever was he going?

'This is awfully queer,' said Julian. 'I'm sure George can't be anywhere in this direction.'

Timmy went on swiftly, occasionally turning his head to make sure everyone was following him. He led the way to the quarry!

'The quarry! Did George come here then?' said Dick. 'But why?'

The dog disappeared down into the middle of the quarry, slipping and sliding down the steep sides as he went. The others followed as best they could. Luckily it was not as slippery as before, and they reached the bottom without accident.

Timmy went straight to the shelf of rock and disappeared underneath it. They heard him give a short sharp bark as if to say 'Come on! This is the way! Hurry up!'

'He's gone into the tunnel under there,' said Dick. 'Where we thought we might explore and didn't. There must be a passage or something there, then. But is George there?'

'I'll go first,' said Julian, and wriggled through the hole. He was soon in the wider bit and then came out into the part where he could almost stand. He walked a little way in the dark, hearing Timmy bark impatiently now and then. But in a moment or two Julian stopped.

'It's no good trying to follow you in the dark, Timmy!' he called. 'We'll have to go back and get torches. I can't see a foot in front of me!'

Dick was just wriggling through the first part of the hole. Julian called to him to go back.

'It's too dark,' he said. 'We must go and get torches. If George for some reason is up this passage, she must have had an accident, and we'd better get a rope, and some brandy.'

Anne began to cry. She didn't like the idea of George lying hurt in that dark passage. Julian put his arm round her as soon as he was in the open air again. He helped her up the sides of the quarry, followed by Dick.

'Now don't worry. We'll get her all right. But it beats me why she went there—and I still can't imagine how Tim and she came from the island, if they are here, instead of on the beach!'

'Look—there's Martin!' suddenly said Dick in surprise So there was! He was standing at the top of the quarry, and seemed just as surprised to see them as they were to see him!

'You're up early,' called Dick. 'And goodness me—are you going gardening or something! Why the spades?'

Martin looked sheepish and didn't seem to know what to say. Julian suddenly walked up to him and caught hold of his shoulder. 'Look here, Martin! There's some funny business going on here! What are going to do with those spades? Have you seen George? Do you know where she is, or anything about her? Come on, tell me!'

Martin shook his shoulder away from Julian's grip looking extremely surprised.

'George? No! What's happened to him?'

'George isn't a him—she's a her,' said Anne, still crying. 'She disappeared. We thought she'd gone to the island to find her dog—and Timmy suddenly appeared at Kirrin Cottage, and brought us here!'

'So it looks as if George might be somewhere near here,' said Julian, 'And I want to know if you've seen her or know anything of her whereabouts?'

'No Julian. I swear I don't!' said Martin.

'Well, tell me what you're doing here so early in the morning, with spades,' said Julian, roughly. 'Who are you waiting for? Your father?'

'Yes,' said Martin.

'And what are you going to do?' asked Dick. 'Going exploring up the hole there?'

'Yes,' said Martin again, sullen and worried. 'No harm in that, is there?'

'It's all—very—queer,' said Julian, eyeing him and speaking slowly and loudly. 'But—let me tell you this—*we're* going exploring —not you! If there's anything queer up that hole, *we'll* find it! We shall not allow you or your father to get through the hole. So go and find him and tell him that!'

Julian suddenly walked up to him and caught hold of his shoulder.

Martin didn't move. He went very white, and stared at Julian miserably. Anne went up to him, tears still on her face and put her hand on his arm.

'Martin, what is it? Why do you look like that? What's the mystery?'

And then, to the dismay and horror of everyone, Martin turned away with a noise that sounded very like a sob! He stood with his back to them, and his shoulders were shaking.

He stood with his back to them, his shoulders shaking.

'Good gracious! What *is* up?' said Julian, in exasperation. 'Pull yourself together, Martin! Tell us what's worrying you.'

'Everything, everything!' said Martin, in a muffled voice. Then he swung round to face them. 'You don't know what it is to have no mother and no father—nobody who cares about you—and then . . .'

'But you *have* got a father!' said Dick at once.

'I haven't. He's not my father, that man. He's only my guardian, but he makes me call him father whenever we're on a job together.'

'A job? What sort of job?' said Julian.

'Oh any kind—all beastly,' said Martin. 'Snooping round and finding things out about people, and then getting money from them if we promise to say nothing—and receiving stolen goods and selling them—and helping people like the men who are after your uncle's secret . . .'

'Oho!' said Dick at once. 'Now we're coming to it. I *thought* you and Mr Curton were both suspiciously interested in Kirrin Island. What's this present job, then?'

'My guardian will half-kill me for telling all this,' said Martin. 'But, you see, they're planning to blow up the island—and it's about the worst thing I've ever been mixed up in—and I know your uncle is there—and perhaps George too now, you say. I can't go on with it!'

A few more tears ran down his cheeks. It was awful to see a boy crying like that, and the three felt sorry for Martin now. They were also full of horror when they heard him say that the island was to be blown up!

'How do you know this?' asked Julian.

'Well, Mr Curton's got a wireless receiver and transmitter as you know,' explained Martin, 'and so have the fellows on the island—the ones who are after your uncle's secret—so they can easily keep in touch with one another. They mean to get the secret if they can—if not they are going to blow the whole place sky-high so that *nobody* can get the secret. But they can't get away by boat because they don't know the way through those rocks . . .'

'My guardian will half-kill me for telling all this,' said Martin. 'But you see they're planning to blow up the island.'

'Well, how will they get away then?' demanded Julian.

'We feel sure this hole that Timmy found the other day, leads down to the sea, and under the sea-bed to Kirrin Island,' said Martin. 'Yes, I know it sounds too mad to be true—but Mr Curton's got an old map which clearly shows there was once a passage under the sea-bed. If there is—well, the fellows across on the island can escape down it, after making all preparations for the island to be blown up. See?'

'Yes,' said Julian, taking a long breath. 'I *do* see. I see it all very clearly now. I see something else too! *Timmy* has found his way from the island, using that same passage you have just told us about—and *that's* why he's led us back here—to take us to the island and rescue Uncle Quentin and George.'

There was a deep silence. Martin stared at the ground. Dick and Julian thought hard. Anne sobbed a little. It all seemed quite unbelievable to her. Then Julian put his hand on Martin's arm.

'Martin! You did right to tell us. We may be able to prevent something dreadful. But you must help. We may need those spades of yours—and I expect you've got torches too. We haven't. We don't want to waste time going back and getting them—so will you come with us and help us? Will you lend us those spades and torches?'

'Would you trust me?' said Martin, in a low voice. 'Yes, I want to come and help you. And if we get in now, my guardian won't be able to follow, because he won't have a torch. We can get to the island and bring your uncle and George safely back.'

'Good for you!' said Dick. 'Well, come on then. We've been talking far too long. Come on down again, Ju. Hand him a spade and a torch, Martin.'

'Anne you're not to come,' said Julian to his little sister. 'You're to go back and tell Aunt Fanny what's happened. Will you do that?'

'Yes. I don't want to come,' said Anne. 'I'll go back now. Do be careful, Julian!'

She climbed down with the boys and then stood and watched till all three had disappeared into the hole. Timmy, who had been waiting impatiently during the talking, barking now and again, was glad to find that at last they were going to make a move. He ran ahead in the tunnel, his eyes gleaming green every time he turned to see if they were following.

Anne began to climb up the steep side of the quarry again. Then, thinking she heard a cough, she stopped and crouched under a bush. She peered through the leaves and saw Mr Curton. Then she heard his voice.

'Martin! Where on earth are you?'

So he had come to look for Martin and go up the tunnel with him! Anne hardly dared to breathe. Mr

Curton called again and again, then made an impatient noise and began to climb down the side of the quarry.

Suddenly he slipped! He clutched at a bush as he passed, but it gave way. He rolled quite near Anne, and caught sight of her. He looked astonished, but then his look became one of fear as he rolled more and more quickly to the bottom of the deep quarry. Anne heard him give a deep groan as at last he came to a stop.

Anne peered down in fright. Mr Curton was sitting up, holding one of his legs and groaning. He looked up to see if he could spy Anne.

'Anne!' he called. 'I've broken my leg, I think. Can you fetch help? What are you doing here so early? Have you seen Martin?'

Anne did not answer. If he had broken his leg, then he couldn't go after the others! And Anne could get away quickly. She climbed carefully, afraid of rolling down to the bottom, and having to lie beside the horrid Mr Curton.

'Anne! Have you seen Martin? Look for him and get help for me, will you?' shouted Mr Curton, and then groaned again.

Anne climbed to the top of the quarry and looked down. She cupped her hands round her mouth and shouted loudly:

'You're a very wicked man. I shan't fetch help for you. I simply can't *bear* you!'

And, having got all that off her chest, the little girl shot off at top speed over the moor.

'I must tell Aunt Fanny. She'll know what to do! Oh I hope the others are safe. What shall we do if the island blows up? I'm glad, glad, glad I told Mr Curton he was a very wicked man.'

And on she ran, panting. Aunt Fanny would know what to do!

Suddenly he slipped!

Chapter 20

Everything boils up

Meanwhile the three boys and Timmy were having a strange journey underground. Timmy led the way without faltering, stopping every now and again for the others to catch up with him.

The tunnel at first had a very low roof and the boys had to walk along in a stooping position, which was very tiring indeed. But after a bit the roof became higher and Julian, flashing his torch round, saw that the walls and floor, instead of being made of soil, were now made of rock. He tried to reckon out where they were.

'We've come practically straight towards the cliff,' he said to Dick. 'That's allowing for a few turns and twists. The tunnel has sloped down so steeply the last few hundred yards that I think we must be very far underground indeed.'

It was not until the boys heard the curious booming noise that George had heard in the caves, that they knew they must be under the rocky bed of the sea. They were walking under the sea to Kirrin Island. How strange, how unbelievably astonishing!

'It's like a peculiarly vivid dream,' said Julian. 'I'm not sure I like it very much! All right Tim—we're coming. Hallo—what's this?'

They all stopped. Julian flashed his torch ahead and saw a pile of fallen rocks. Timmy had managed to squeeze himself through a hole in them and go through to the other side, but the boys couldn't.

'This is where the spades come in, Martin!' said Dick, cheerfully. 'Take a hand!'

By dint of pushing and shovelling, the boys at last managed to move the pile of fallen rocks enough to make a way past. 'Thank goodness for the spades!' said Julian.

They went on, and were soon very glad of the spades again, to move another heap of rock. Timmy barked impatiently when they kept him waiting. He was very anxious to get back to George.

Soon they came to where the tunnel forked into two. But Timmy took the right-hand passage without hesitation, and when that one forked into three, he again chose one without stopping to think for a moment.

'Marvellous, isn't he?' said Julian. 'All done by smell! He's been this way once, so he knows it again. We should be completely lost under here if we came by ourselves.'

Martin was not enjoying this adventure at all. He said very little, but laboured on after the others. Dick guessed he was worrying about what was going to happen when the adventure was over. Poor Martin. All he wanted to do was to draw—and instead of that he had been dragged into one horrible job after another, and used as a cat's-paw by his evil guardian.

'Do you think we're anywhere near the island?' said Dick, at last. 'I'm getting tired of this!'

'It's like a peculiarly vivid dream,' said Julian. 'I'm not sure I like it very much.'

'Yes, we must be,' said Julian. 'In fact I think we'd better be as quiet as we can, in case we come suddenly on the enemy!'

So, without speaking again, they went as quietly as they could—and then suddenly they saw a faint light ahead of them. Julian put out his hand to stop the others.

They were nearing the cave where George's father had his books and papers—where George had found him the night before. Timmy stood in front of them, listening too. He was not going to run headlong into danger!

They heard voices, and listened intently to see whose they were. 'George's—and Uncle Quentin's,' said Julian at last. And as if Timmy had also satisfied himself that those were indeed the two voices, the dog ran ahead and went into the lighted cave, barking joyfully.

'Timmy!' came George's voice, and they heard something overturn as she sprang up. 'Where have you been?'

'Woof,' said Timmy, trying to explain. 'Woof!'

And then Julian and Dick ran into the cave followed by Martin! Uncle Quentin and George stared in the very greatest amazement.

'Julian! Dick! And *Martin*! How did *you* get here?' cried George, while Timmy jumped and capered round her.

'I'll explain,' said Julian. 'It was Timmy that fetched us!' And he related the whole story of how Timmy had come into Kirrin Cottage in the early morning and had jumped on his bed, and all that had happened since.

And then, in their turn, Uncle Quentin and George told all that had happened to *them*!

'Where are the two men?' asked Julian.

'Somewhere on the island,' said George. 'I went scouting after them some time ago, and followed them up to where they get out into the little stone room. I think they're

'Julian! Dick! And Martin! How did you get here?'

there until half past ten, when they'll go up and signal, so that people will think everything is all right.'

'Well, what are our plans?' said

Julian. 'Will you come back down the passage under the sea with us? Or what shall we do?'

'Better not do that,' said Martin, quickly. 'My guardian may be coming—and he's in touch with other men. If he wonders where I am, and thinks something is up, he may call in two or three others, and we might meet them making their way up the passage.'

They did not know, of course, that Mr Curton was even then lying with a broken leg at the bottom of the quarry. Uncle Quentin considered.

'I've been given seven hours to say whether or not I will give the fellows my secret,' he said. 'That time will be up just after half past ten. Then the men will come down again to see me. I think between us we ought to be able to capture them—especially as we've got Timmy with us!'

In vain Uncle Quentin swung the lever to and fro. Nothing happened.

'Yes—that's a good idea,' said Julian. 'We could hide somewhere till they come—and then set Timmy on them before they suspect anything!'

Almost before he had finished these words the light in the cave went out! Then a voice spoke out of the blackness.

'Keep still! One movement and I'll shoot.'

George gasped. What was happening? Had the men come back unexpectedly? Oh, why hadn't Timmy given them warning? She had been fondling his ears, so probably he had been unable to hear anything!

She held Timmy's collar, afraid that he would fly at the man in the darkness and be shot. The voice spoke again.

'Will you or will you not give us your secret?'

'No,' said Uncle Quentin in a low voice.

'You will have this whole island, and all your work blown up then, and yourself too and the others?'

'Yes! You can do what you like!' suddenly yelled George. 'You'll be blown up yourself too. You'll never be able to get away in a boat—you'll go on the rocks!'

The man in the darkness laughed. 'We shall be safe,' he said. 'Now keep at the back of the cave. I have you covered with my revolver.'

They all crouched at the back. Timmy growled, but George made him stop at once. She did not know if the men knew he was free or not.

Quiet footsteps passed across the cave in the darkness. George listened, straining her ears. Two pairs of footsteps! Both men were passing through the cave. She knew where they were going! They were going to escape by the undersea passage—and leave the island to be blown up behind them!

As soon as the footsteps had died away, George switched on her torch. 'Father! Those men are escaping now, down the sea-tunnel. We must escape too—but not that way. My boat is on the shore. Let's get there quickly and get away before there's any explosion.'

'Yes, come along,' said her father. 'But if only I could get up into my tower, I could stop any wicked plan of theirs! They mean to use the power there. I know—but if I could get up to the glass room, I could undo all their plans!'

'Oh do be quick then, Father!' cried George, getting in quite a panic now. 'Save my island if you can!'

They all made their way through the cave up to the pasage that led to the stone flight of steps from the little stone room. And there they had a shock!

The stone could not be opened from the inside! The men had altered the mechanism so that it could now only be opened from the outside.

In vain Uncle Quentin swung the lever to and fro. Nothing happened. The stone would not move.

'It's only from outside it can be opened,' he said in despair. 'We're trapped!'

They sat down on the stone steps in a row, one above the other. They were cold, hungry and miserable. What could they do now? Make their way back to the cave, and then go on down the under-sea tunnel?

'I don't want to do that,' said Uncle Quentin. 'I'm so afraid that if there is an explosion, it may crack the rocky bed of the sea, which is the roof of the tunnel—and then water would pour in. It wouldn't be pleasant if we happened to be there at that moment.'

'Oh no. Don't let's be trapped like that,' said George with a shudder. 'I couldn't bear it.'

'Perhaps I could get something to explode this stone away,' said her father, after a while. 'I've got plenty of stuff if only I've time to put it together.'

'Listen!' said Julian, suddenly. 'I can hear something outside this wall. Sh!'

They all listened intently. Timmy whined and scratched at the stone that would not move.

'It's voices!' cried Dick. 'Lots of them. Who can it be?'

'Be *quiet*,' said Julian, fiercely. 'We *must* find out!'

'I know, I know!' said George, suddenly. 'It's the fishermen who have come over in their boats! *That's* why they've gone in such a hurry! They must have seen the fisher-boats coming!'

'Then Anne must have brought them!' cried Dick. 'She must have run home to Aunt Fanny, told her everything and given the news to the fishermen—and they've come to rescue us! Anne! ANNE! WE'RE HERE!'

Timmy began to bark deafeningly. The others encouraged him, because they felt certain that Timmy's bark would be louder than their shouts!

'WOOF! WOOF! WOOF!'

Anne heard the barking and the shouting as soon as she ran into the little stone room. 'Where are you? Where are you?' she yelled.

'HERE! HERE! MOVE THE STONE!' yelled Julian, shouting so loudly that everyone near him jumped violently.

'Move aside, miss—I can see which stone it is,' said a man's deep voice. It was one of the fishermen. He felt round and about the stone in the recess, sure it was the right one because it was cleaner than the others through being used as an entrance.

Suddenly he touched the right place, and found a tiny iron spike. He pulled it down—and the lever swung back behind it, and pulled the stone aside!

Everyone hurried out, one on top of the other! The six fishermen standing in the little room stared in astonishment. Aunt Fanny was there too, and Anne. Aunt Fanny ran to her husband as soon as he appeared—but to her surprise he pushed her away quite roughly.

He ran out of the room, and hurried to the tower. Was he in time to save the island and everyone on it? Oh hurry, hurry!

'Move aside, miss—I can see which stone it is,' said a man's deep voice.

Puzzle Answers

Island Quiz

1. Brownsea, in Poole Harbour. 2. 140. 3. Jersey, Guernsey, Alderney and Sark. 4. Harris. 5. Tristan da Cunha, in the South Atlantic. 6. The Isle of Man. 7. Easter Island. 8. Trinidad. 9. Scilly Isles. 10. Iona. 11. Caldey Island. 12. Jamaica. 13. Isle of Wight. 14. Greenland. 15. No — it is a peninsula. 16. Komodo — in the East Indies. 17. A prison settlement. 18. Ireland. 19. St. Helena. 20. Juan Fernandez, South America.

Musical Mix-Up

1. Violin. 2. Guitar. 3. Piano. 4. Banjo. 5. Organ. 6. Accordion. 7. Trumpet. 8. Trombone. 9. Flute. 10. Cello.

Animals in Your Garden

1. Dragon. 2. Fox. 3. Lion. 4. Cow. 5. Pussy. 6. Dog. 7. Tiger. 8. Cat. 9. Goose. 10. Chick.

Word Diamond

D
SIP
SPARE
DIAMOND
PROUD
END
D

Time for Thought

(A) Eleven times

(B) The power was off for 7½ hours. It came back on at 12 midnight.

A Postal Problem

Dudley Underwood Esquire
Andover
Hampshire

Game Scrabble

1. Polo. 2. Croquet. 3. Golf. 4. Cricket. 5. Chess. 6. Football. 7. Tennis. 8. Hockey. 9. Rugby. 10. Badminton. 11. Draughts. 12. Whist.

Public Schools in Hiding

1. Winchester. 2. Harrow. 3. Lancing. 4. Rugby. 5. Wellington.

Sea and Seaside Quiz

1. Southend, 1½ miles. 2. Blackpool. 3. Puffins. 4. Cormorant. 5. Punch and Judy. 6. Quay. 7. Sargasso. 8. Limpets. 9. Some can give a painful sting. 10. The Dead Sea. 11. Lulworth. 12. Storm Petrels. 13. White cliffs. 14. Skeletons of marine animals. 15. Donkey. 16. The Needles, off the Isle of Wight. 17. The Gulf of Mexico. 18. Seaside rock. 19. Pacific, Atlantic, Indian, Arctic. 20. No. It is a marine animal found in rock pools.

General Knowledge Crossword Puzzle Answers

ACROSS: 1. Gnu; 3. Sty; 5. Elder; 6. Damp; 7. Tea; 9. Ash; 11. Lost; 13. Thor; 15. Up; 17. Romeo; 19. Spaniel; 20. Seed.

DOWN: 1. Go; 2. Alp; 3. Set; 4. Trent; 5. Emu; 6. Dash; 8. Rouen; 9. Atom; 10. Horse; 12. Spoil; 14. Rope; 16. Well; 18. Mad.

Chapter 21

The end of the adventure

WELL—THANKS. IF YOU CAN GET ME AWAY FROM MY GUARDIAN—AND NEVER LET ME SEE HIM AGAIN—I'D BE QUITE HAPPY!
I DON'T THINK YOU NEED WORRY. IT'S QUITE LIKELY THAT MR. CURTON WILL BE PUT SOMEWHERE SAFE AFTER THIS. I DOUBT IF YOU'LL BE SEEING HIM FOR A VERY LONG TIME!
AS SOON AS THE BOATS REACHED SHORE, JULIAN, DICK, TIMMY AND UNCLE QUENTIN WENT OFF TO THE QUARRY...
WE KNOW YOUR PART IN THIS, CURTON. YOU WILL BE DEALT WITH BY THE POLICE. THEY WILL BE ALONG IN A SHORT WHILE. MEANWHILE, WE'RE GOING TO LIE IN WAIT FOR YOUR TWO FRIENDS.
AN HOUR WENT BY, BUT THERE WAS NO SIGN OF THE TWO MEN. THEN THE POLICE ARRIVED, ALONG WITH A POLICE DOCTOR WHO SAW TO MR. CURTON'S LEG...
WE'LL TAKE OVER HERE, SIR, IF YOU WANTED TO BE OFF HOME.
DEAR ME, NO! I WANT TO SEE THE FACES OF THESE TWO FELLOWS WHEN THEY COME OUT. THE ISLAND IS SAFE, AS IS MY SECRET. AND I JUST WANT TO TELL MY TWO DEAR FRIENDS.
THEY SETTLED DOWN TO WAIT AGAIN WHILE JULIAN WENT OFF TO FETCH SOME SANDWICHES AND COFFEE...
YOU KNOW, FATHER, I BELIEVE THEY'VE LOST THEIR WAY UNDERGROUND. JULIAN SAID THERE WERE MANY DIFFERENT PASSAGES.
YES. TIMMY TOOK US THROUGH THE RIGHT ONES, OF COURSE—BUT WE WOULD HAVE BEEN LOST IF WE HADN'T HAD HIM WITH US.
WAIT—WE COULD SEND TIMMY IN! HE WOULD SOON FIND THEM AND BRING THEM OUT. WOULDN'T YOU, TIM?
YES! THEY WOULDN'T HURT HIM IF THEY THOUGHT HE COULD SHOW THEM THE WAY OUT! GO ON, TIMMY—FIND THEM! BRING THEM HERE!
WOOF!
JULIAN RETURNED WITH THE FOOD, AND THEY ALL SAT MUNCHING SANDWICHES AND SIPPING COFFEE WHILE TIMMY SOUGHT OUT THE TWO LOST MEN. THEN...
LISTEN—I CAN HEAR TIMMY BARKING! HE MUST HAVE FOUND THEM!
AND VERY SOON...
GOOD MORNING, JOHNSON... PETERS. HOW ARE YOU? DID YOU ENJOY YOUR UNDERGROUND WALK? WE FOUND IT BETTER TO COME BY SEA.
ALL RIGHT—IT'S ALL UP. YOU WIN!
I DO. IN FACT, I WIN HANDSOMELY. YOUR LITTLE PLAN WENT WRONG. MY SECRET IS STILL SAFE—AND NEXT YEAR IT WILL BE GIVEN TO THE WHOLE WORLD!
GOOD OLD TIMMY! I BET THEY WERE GLAD WHEN YOU CAME UP TO THEM!
YES. WE WERE LOST IN THOSE HATEFUL TUNNELS. CURTON SAID HE'D COME TO MEET US, BUT HE NEVER CAME.

NO. HE'S PROBABLY IN THE PRISON HOSPITAL BY NOW, WITH A BROKEN LEG. WELL, CONSTABLE— DO YOUR DUTY.
THE TWO MEN WERE ARRESTED, AND THEN THE WHOLE COMPANY MADE THEIR WAY BACK OVER THE MOOR. THE CHILDREN AND UNCLE QUENTIN WATCHED AS THE POLICEMEN AND THEIR PRISONERS DROVE AWAY, AND THEN THEY WENT INTO KIRRIN COTTAGE FOR A GOOD MEAL!
I'M MOST TERRIBLY HUNGRY! JOANNA, HAVE YOU GOT ANYTHING NICE FOR BREAKFAST?
NOT MUCH— ONLY BACON AND EGGS AND MUSHROOMS!
OOOH! JOANNA, YOU SHALL HAVE THE O.B.C.B.E.!
AND WHAT MAY THAT BE?
ANNE COULDN'T REMEMBER EXACTLY WHAT THOSE LETTERS STOOD FOR...
ER, IT'S A DECORATION!
WELL, I'M NOT A CHRISTMAS TREE! YOU COME AND HELP WITH THE BREAKFAST!
IT WAS A JOLLY BREAKFAST THAT THEY ALL SAT DOWN TO. MARTIN, NOW THAT HE WAS FREE OF HIS GUARDIAN, BECAME QUITE A DIFFERENT BOY...
YOU CAN STAY WITH THE COASTGUARD, BECAUSE HE LIKES YOU!
AND YOU CAN COME AND PLAY WITH US AND GO TO THE ISLAND!
AND UNCLE QUENTIN WILL SEE IF HE CAN GET YOU INTO AN ART-SCHOOL. HE SAYS YOU DESERVE A REWARD FOR HELPING TO SAVE HIS WONDERFUL SECRET!
I-I'VE NEVER HAD A CHANCE TILL NOW. I'LL MAKE GOOD. YOU SEE IF I DON'T!
MOTHER! CAN WE GO AND STAY ON KIRRIN ISLAND AND WATCH THE TOWER BEING TAKEN DOWN TOMORROW? DO SAY YES! AND CAN WE STAY THERE A WHOLE WEEK?
WELL— I SUPPOSE YOU CAN! I'D RATHER LIKE TO HAVE YOUR FATHER TO MYSELF FOR A FEW DAYS AND FEED HIM UP A BIT.
OH— THAT REMINDS ME, FANNY... I TRIED SOME SOUP YOU LEFT FOR ME, THE NIGHT BEFORE LAST. AND MY DEAR, IT WAS HORRIBLE! QUITE BAD!
OH QUENTIN! I TOLD YOU TO POUR IT AWAY! YOU KNOW I DID! IT MUST HAVE BEEN COMPLETELY BAD. YOU REALLY ARE DREADFUL!
THEY ALL FINISHED THEIR BREAKFAST AT LAST, AND WENT OUT INTO THE GARDEN...
OH LOOK AT KIRRIN ISLAND! ISN'T IT LOVELY IN THE MORNING SUN!
WE'VE HAD A LOT OF ADVENTURES TOGETHER. MORE THAN MOST CHILDREN. THEY HAVE BEEN EXCITING, HAVEN'T THEY?
YES— THEY HAVE, BUT NOW WE MUST SAY GOODBYE TO THE FIVE, AND TO KIRRIN ISLAND TOO. GOODBYE, JULIAN, DICK, GEORGE, ANNE— AND TIMMY. BUT ONLY TIMMY HEARS OUR GOODBYE, FOR HE HAS SUCH SHARP EARS.